DOORS

Excellence in international design

Gretl Hoffmann

DOORS
Excellence in international design

George Godwin Limited — London
The Whitney Library of Design — New York

Library of Congress Cataloging in Publication Data

Hoffmann, Gretl, 1925—
    Doors.

    First published under title: Dekorative Türen.
    English and German.
    1. Doors.   2. Decoration and ornament.   I. Title.
NA3000.H6313   729'.38   77-23807
ISBN 0-8230-7135-9

First published 1977 in West Germany by Julius
Hoffmann Verlag, Pfizerstrasse 5-7, 7000 Stuttgart 1

First published 1977 in Great Britain by George
Godwin Limited, The book publishing subsidiary of
The Builder Group, 2-4 Catherine Street, London WC2

ISBN 0 7114 3414 X

First published 1978 in the United States by Whitney
Library of Design, an imprint of Watson-Guptill
Publications, a division of Billboard Publications
Inc. 1515 Broadway, New York, New York 10036

Printed in West Germany. Bound in Great Britain.

Inhalt

Contents

Vorwort

Jede Tür ist Abgrenzung und Verschluß, zugleich aber auch Verbindung zwischen außen und innen. Haustüren mußten von jeher besonders stabil sein. Aufdoppelungen gaben ihnen die notwendige Widerstandskraft, verlockten aber auch zum Spiel mit dem Ornament. Zeichen und Symbole auf dem Türblatt oder auf der Türumrahmung deuteten schon vor Jahrhunderten an, was hinter der Tür liegt.

Künstlerischen Schmuck hatte die Moderne zunächst vor allem dem Kirchenbau vorbehalten. Im sakralen Bereich spielt die Tür als Zutritt zu einer anderen Welt eine besondere Rolle. Doch auch im Profanbau weicht heute das glatte abgesperrte Türblatt oder die einfache Metall-Glas-Konstruktion bewegteren, individuelleren Lösungen. Neben das anonyme Industrieerzeugnis tritt immer häufiger die speziell entworfene Tür.

Auch innerhalb des Gebäudes beginnen wir, mit der Konstruktion und dem Aussehen der Tür zu spielen. Farben und Formen übernehmen Hinweisfunktionen, die zu leiten oder auch zu warnen vermögen. Die Tür wird zum durchschreitbaren Zeichen. Aus dem Bauprinzip lassen sich Formsysteme entwickeln, so daß Konstruktion und Ornament eins werden.

Ob Farbe und Form bei der Tür rein als Dekor aufgefaßt sind oder ob sie als Hinweise fungieren, in jedem Fall muß die Tür richtig und stabil gebaut und zuverlässig angeschlagen sein. Beim Entwurf einer Eingangstür ist zudem an Klingel- und Sprechanlage, an Briefkasten und dergleichen zu denken. Der funktionsgerechte Verschluß ist zu wählen, vom auch für Zimmertüren möglichen Magnetverschluß bis zum aufbohrsicheren Zylinder einer Schließanlage.

Auf solche konstruktiven Erfordernisse geht dieses Buch nicht ein, wenn sie auch von Fall zu Fall einmal im Text angesprochen sind. Wir wollten vielmehr zeigen, was heute zur Gestaltung und zum Schmuck einer Tür an Mitteln verfügbar ist, und damit Anregungen für weitere schöpferische Entwicklungen auf diesem reizvollen Gebiet geben.

Preface

Every door is at once a boundary, shutting off one area from another, and also a bond between the inside and the outside. Throughout the ages entrance doors to buildings have always had to be exceptionally robust. Batten construction conferred on them the necessary strength, but it also provided interesting scope for decoration. Signs and symbols already appeared centuries ago to furnish an indication of what lay behind the door. Ornamentation of doors in modern times is a special feature of church architecture. In the realm of the sacred, the door has a special role as a threshold to the world beyond. In the secular field too however, the plain, flush door or the simple metal-glass system are giving way to livelier and more original designs. Individually created doors are increasingly found beside the anonymous factory product.

Now we are beginning to experiment with the structure and aesthetic appearance of interior doors in buildings as well. Forms and colours assume indicative functions — they give directions or warnings. According to the particular architectural principle adopted, formal systems are devised so that structure and decoration are one.

Whatever the role of colour and form in the door, whether conceived purely as decoration or to carry a message, the door construction itself must be sound and strongly built with an efficient closing system. In planning the front door, the door-bell, the intercom, the letter-box and other fittings have also to be considered. The lock selected must be the most suitable for the purpose, whether a magnetic catch for internal doors or a burglar-proof cylinder fitting for a safety installation.

The present work will not go into details regarding these design accessories, although occasional mention is made of them in the text. It is rather our aim to show the range of possibilities existing for the formal design and decoration of doors today and to provide inspiration for creative development in the future.

Fotografen

Seitenportale der kath. Kirche St. Elisabeth, Freiburg. Einflügelige Tür 1,00 × 1,98 m in Grauguß. Plattendicke 19 mm; oben, unten und auf der Bandseite verstärkt. Die Türen sind mit schweren angegossenen Bändern (⌀ 80 mm) an die ebenfalls gegossene Wandplatte 1,85 × 2,40 m angeschlagen. Die Darstellung nimmt Bezug auf die Legende der Hl. Elisabeth: Das eine Feld zeigt Rosen, das andere ihre Verwandlung in Brot.

Bildhauer Franz Gutmann, Münstertal
Architekt Rainer Disse, Karlsruhe

Side portals of the Roman Catholic Church of St. Elisabeth, Freiburg. Single-leaf door, 1.00 × 1.98 m, in grey cast iron. Panel thickness 19 mm, reinforced at top, bottom and hinge side. The doors have heavy, integrally cast iron hinges (dia. 80 mm), closing on to similar cast iron wall panels, 1.85 × 2.40 m. The decorative motifs relate to the Legend of Saint Elisabeth: one bay shows roses, the other their transformation into bread.

Hauptportal der kath. Kirche St. Elisabeth, Freiburg. Grauguß. Flügelmaße 1,25 × 2,36 m. Der Türverschluß wird hier gleichzeitig als Türgriff verwendet. Angegossene Zapfenbänder. Innenliegender Treibriegel und BKS-Schloß.
Bildhauer Franz Gutmann, Münstertal
Architekt Rainer Disse, Karlsruhe

Main portal of the R. Cath. Church of St. Elisabeth, Freiburg. Grey cast iron. Wing dimensions 1.25 × 2.36 m. The door latch here also acts as handle. Integrally cast mortise hinges. Cremorne bolts and cylindrical lock on the interior.

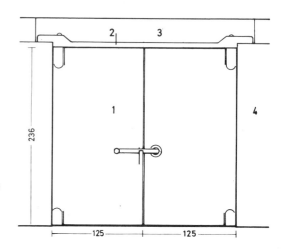

Ansicht 1:50	Elevation 1:50
1 Türflügel mit angegossenen Lagern	1 Door leaf with integrally cast supports
2 gegossener Kämpfer	2 Cast transom
3 Verglasung	3 Glazing
4 Sichtbeton	4 Fair-faced concrete

Nebeneingang der kath. Kirche St. Elisabeth, Freiburg. Er ist als kräftig gewölbte Schale in Grauguß ausgebildet. Zapfenlager in der oberen und unteren Kantenfläche, vgl. Detailfoto. Größe 1,30 × 2,30 m. Äußerer Türgriff angegossen, innerer Griff geschmiedet; im Sichtfeld eine Gußglasscheibe.

Bildhauer Franz Gutmann, Münstertal
Architekt Rainer Disse, Karlsruhe

Side entrance to R. Cath. Church of St. Elisabeth, Freiburg, designed as a boldly curved shell in grey cast iron. Mortise cases in the upper and lower edge zones, cf. detail photo. Dimensions 1.30 × 2.30 m. External door grip integrally cast, interior handle of wrought iron; a cast glass pane in the viewing panel.

Christ-König-Kirche, Eppelheim. Hauptportal. Die vier Türflügel sind aus Eisen gegossen (Grauguß) und messen 1,00 × 2,74 m. Türblattdicke etwa 2 cm, Gewicht eines Flügels etwa 450 kp. Über die beiden linken Türflügel zieht sich diagonal eine Darstellung des Guten Hirten. Die symbolischen Darstellungen der oberen Türfelder (Hand Gottes, Taube, Weltkugel, Tiara, Mitra) sind ebenso wie die Türgriffe mit Plexiglasschalen hinterlegt. Die Türen laufen in angegossenen Zapfenbändern. Rechts der Gehflügel. Verriegelung von innen durch Hoftorriegel.

Bildhauer Franz Gutmann, Münstertal
Architekt Erzbischöfliches Bauamt Heidelberg
(M. Schmitt-Fiebig und H. Eisenhauer)

Church of Christ the King, Eppelheim. Main portal. The four door wings are in cast iron (grey iron), measuring 1.00 × 2.94 m. Door leaf thickness 2 cm approx., weight of one wing about 450 kg. A representation of the Good Shepherd extends diagonally over the two L. H. door leaves. The symbolic designs appearing on the upper door bays (the Hand of God, dove, the globe, tiara, mitre) as well as the door handles have "Perspex" shell backing. The doors operate on integrally cast mortise hinges. On the right: the swing access door leaf. Interior bolting by means of gateway bolts.

Seiteneinang an der Christ-König-Kirche in Eppelheim. Zwei Türflügel in Grauguß. Maße 1,05 × 2,20 m. Die das Türblatt umgebenden Wülste sind an den Ecken so weit herausgezogen, daß sie mit durchgesteckten gegossenen Bolzen das Türlager bilden. Außer der Flügelverriegelung tragen beide Türflügel innen Hoftorriegel, so daß kein Schloß erforderlich ist.

Bildhauer Franz Gutmann, Münstertal
Architekt Erzbischöfliches Bauamt Heidelberg
(M. Schmitt-Fiebig und H. Eisenhauer)

Side entrance to the Church of Christ the King, Eppelheim. Both door wings in grey cast iron. Dimensions 1.05 × 2.20 m. The bead surround is extended at the corners to form the door supports with the cast bolt sockets. As well as the centre (wing) bolt, both door wings have gateway bar bolts on the inside so that no lock is required.

Kirche der Verklärung Christi, Feldberg/Schwarzwald. Die zweiflügeligen Tore sind samt Türlager und Griff aus Stahl gegossen (Sphäroguß). Flügelmaße 1,06 × 2,20 m. Verschluß durch geschmiedeten Drehgriff, nachts Verschluß durch Bodenriegel auf der Innenseite der Tür.
Bildhauer Franz Gutmann, Münstertal
Architekt Rainer Disse, Karlsruhe

Church of Christ's Transfiguration, Feldberg/Schwarzwald. The double-leaf doors together with supports and handle are all in cast steel (spheroidal graphite cast iron). Wing dimensions 1.06 × 2.20 m. Wrought iron door pull, night lock by floor bolts on inside of door.

Eingangstür am Friedhof in Neureut bei Karlsruhe. Selbsttragende Flügel mit kräftiger Profilierung in Grauguß, schwarz gestrichen. Die Tür ist um eine außermittige Achse drehbar, an der ihre beiden Blatthälften zusammengeschraubt sind. Maße der Gußteile etwa 1,40 × 2,20 und 0,80 × 2,20 m. Verschluß durch einen geschmiedeten Fallenriegel.
Bildhauer Peter Dreher, Freiburg
Architekt Rainer Disse, Karlsruhe

Entrance door to the Cemetery of Neureut, near Karlsruhe. Self-supporting wings with bold profiling in grey cast iron, painted black. The door revolves on an eccentric pivot hinge, to which the two half leaves are screwed. Dimensions of the cast iron components approx. 1.40 × 2.20 and 0.80 × 2.20 m. Fastening by means of a wrought-iron drop bolt.

Portal an der Münsterkirche, Mönchengladbach. Die in ein neoromanisches Steingewände eingesetzte Tür ist 1,60 × 2,66 m groß. Sie ist zusammen mit den Beschlägen in Eisenguß (Sphäroguß) gefertigt und mit Naturlack behandelt. Alle Teile sind beweglich. Der Gehflügel hängt am rechten Türteil und ist mit automatischen Türschließern angeschlagen.

Bildhauer Franz Gutmann, Münstertal

Portal of the Minster Church, Moenchengladbach. The door, measuring 1.60 × 2.66 m, is set in a neo-Romanesque masonry architrave. The door and all the fittings are in cast iron, with a natural varnish coating. All components are movable. The swing door is hung on right-hand hinges and has automatic floor closers.

Die beiden Flügel des Türgewändes können nach innen aufgeschlagen werden. Der Gehflügel ist mit angegossenen austragenden Bändern befestigt. Mit angegossen sind ebenfalls die Stoßgriffleisten innen und die Führungen für den Feststellriegel unten.

The two outer wings surrounding the swing door can be opened inwards. The swing door is hung on integrally cast iron, reinforced hinges. The handle mouldings and lip on the interior and the guide straps for the slide bolts beneath are also integrally cast.

Eingangstür an der Versöhnungskirche im ehem. Konzentrationslager Dachau. Das Türblatt besteht aus 4 Platten mit 15 mm dickem rostfreiem Stahl. Sie tragen in Deutsch, Polnisch, Französisch und Niederländisch das Zitat „Zuflucht ist unter dem Schatten Deiner Flügel". Die Buchstaben sind geätzt. Gesamtmaß 280 × 180 cm, Gewicht etwa 580 kg. Außermittige Lagerung durch einen Bodentürschließer in Sonderanfertigung. Das Türblatt ist zwischen 2 Stahlprofile ⊏ 20 eingespannt; Befestigung durch 8 Edelstahl-Schrauben. Die Platten sind grob geschliffen, die Schweißnähte sichtbar aufgetragen.

Bildhauer Fritz Kühn †
Architekt Helmut Striffler, Mannheim

Entrance door to the Church of the Atonement in the former concentration camp of Dachau. The door leaf consists of 4 stainless steel plates, 15 mm thick. They are inscribed, in etched lettering, with the Biblical quotation "Hide me under the shadow of Thy wings", in German, Polish, French and Dutch. Overall dimensions 2.80 × 1.80 m, weight approx. 580 kg. Eccentric base support by means of a specially designed floor closer. The door leaf is hung between two rolled channel steel sections; attachment by 8 stainless steel screws. The plates are rough ground and the seam welds visibly applied.

Tür zur Taufkapelle, kath. Kirche St. Michael in Altenbach. Die beiden Flügel stehen über Eck, sind von innen verriegelt und nach außen zu öffnen. Die Flügel sind ca. 40 mm dick. In dem umlaufenden Rahmen 40/30 mm ist eine starke Stahlblechfüllung befestigt. Darauf sind innen und außen Stahlplatten verschiedener Stärke montiert, die ausgeschnitten und mosaikartig zusammengefügt sind. Ihre Oberfläche ist grob und in wechselnden Richtungen geschliffen, so daß sich die Bildwirkung je nach Lichteinfall verändert. Alle Teile rostfreier Stahl.

Bildhauer Josef Weber, Grötzingen bei Karlsruhe, in Zusammenarbeit mit Guido Messer
Architekt Rainer Disse, Karlsruhe

Door to Baptismal Chapel, R. Cath. Church of St. Michael, Altenbach. The two wings enclosing a corner are bolted on the inside and open outwards. The wings are approx. 40 mm thick. Heavy steel sheet panels are secured to the 40/30 mm frame surround. On these, both inside and out, are mounted steel plate shapes of varying thickness, forming a mosaic. The surface is burnished in alternating directions so that the optical pattern changes with the incidence of the light. All components of stainless steel.

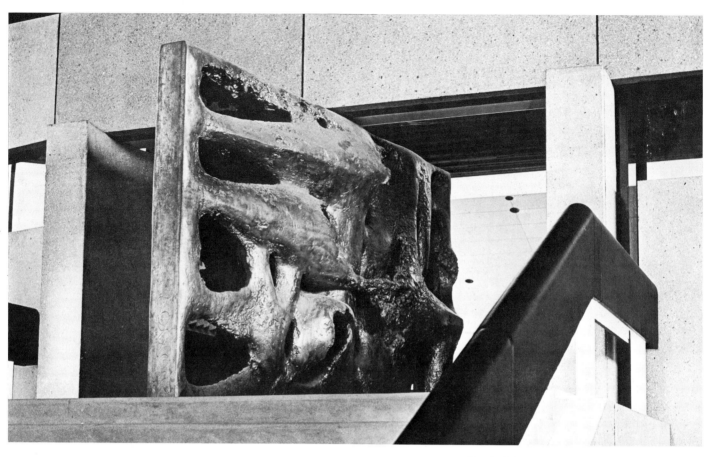

Provinzialverwaltung in 's Hertogenbosch. Eine um ihre Mittelachse drehbare Tür aus Bronzeguß bildet den Zugang zum Großen Sitzungssaal.

Architekten Maaskant, van Dommelen, Kroos und Senf, Rotterdam

Regional administrative office, in 's Hertogenbosch. A cast bronze, revolving door on a central pivot forms the entrance to the Main Council Chamber.

Kapuzinergruft in der Hofburg in Wien. Die beiden Türblätter, jedes etwa 0,80 × 2,20 m groß, sind aus 10 mm dicken Stahlscheiben zusammengesetzt, die durch Autogenschweißen von großen Stahlblöcken abgetrennt wurden und in einen gegliederten Rahmen aus Stahlprofilen eingesetzt sind. Der Stahl zeigt seine bläulichen Anlauffarben. Anschlag mit geschmiedeter Pfanne (unten) und Halsenband (oben).

Bildhauer Rudolf Hoflehner, Wien
Architekt Karl Schwanzer †

Capuchin crypt in the Hofburg, Vienna. The two door leaves, each approx. 0.80 × 2.20 m in size, are composed of 10 mm thick steel plates, oxygen cut from large steel blocks, and set in an articulated, steel sectional grid frame. The steel retains its bluish annealing colour. Socket (below) and collar (above) transom closing.

Portal der Willehadi Kirche, Garbsen bei Hannover. Die Tür ist 2,28 × 2,20 m groß. Jeder Flügel ist mit einer Platte aus Bronzeguß bekleidet. Sie stellen die beiden Gleichnisse vom Gastmahl bei Lukas (Bescheidenheit und Gastfreiheit) dar und nehmen Bezug auf den Hunger in der Welt. Die Flügel haben eine tragende Konstruktion aus Stahlprofilen und sind auf der Innenseite und an den Kanten mit Kupferblech bekleidet. Anschlag mit Zapfenbändern.

Bildhauer Karl Henning Seemann, Löchgau
Architekt Wolfgang Westphal, Bremerhaven

Portal of the Willehadi Church, Garbsen nr. Hanover. Door measurement: 2.28 × 2.20 m. Each wing has a cast bronze cladding panel. These represent the two parables at the Great Supper in St. Luke's Gospel (humility and hospitality) and relate to famine in the world. The wings are constructed of loadbearing steel sections with copper sheet cladding on the interior and edges. Hanging stile with mortise hinges.

Die 2,45 × 4,00 m große Bronzetür an der Barockkirche St. Jacobi in Hamburg sollte eine nicht mehr vorhandene, ursprünglich holzgeschnitzte Tür ersetzen. Es wird hier die Lebensgeschichte des Hl. Jacobus gezeigt. Gegenüber dem räumlich gestalteten Tympanon, das das Weltgericht darstellt, erscheinen die Türen flächig, gobelinartig. Die in Bronze gegossenen Tafeln (Wachsausschmelzverfahren) sind auf eine Unterkonstruktion aus Eichenholz geschraubt. Befestigung mit Zapfenbändern; oben schlagen die Türblätter am Architrav des Tympanon an.

Bildhauer Jürgen Weber, Braunschweig

The 2.45 × 4.00 m bronze door to the Baroque Church of St. James, Hamburg, replaces an original carved wooden door no longer in existence. It portrays the life of St. James. In contrast to the generous tympanon depicting the Day of Judgment, the doors take the form of drapes, or tapestries. The cast bronze bays (lost wax process) are screwed into a wooden sub-structure of oak. Hung on mortise hinges; the door leaves above close on to the architrave of the tympanon.

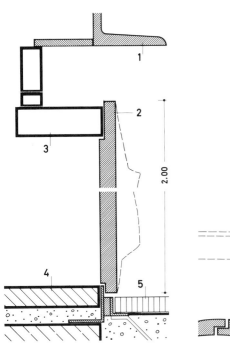

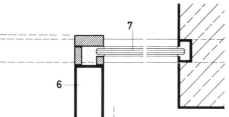

Kirche der Gute Hirte, Friedrichshafen. Die beiden Türblätter sind vollplastisch in Aluminium gegossen. Die Griffe sind als Mulden ausgebildet.

Bildhauer Erich Hauser, Rottweil

Architekt Wilfried Beck-Erlang, Stuttgart

Church of the Good Shepherd, Friedrichshafen. The two door leaves are cast as sculptured aluminium. The handles are of trough design.

Schnitte 1:5

1   U-Profil 28/10 cm
2   Türblatt Aluminiumguß, 20–80 mm dick
3   Stahlrohr 120/40/3 mm
4   Plattenbelag
5   Abtretmatte
6   Stahlrohr 80/40/3 mm
7   Spiegelglas, vorgespannt

Sections 1:5

1   Rolled channel section 28/10 cm
2   Door leaf in cast aluminium, 20–80 mm thick
3   Tubular steel 120/40/3 mm
4   Floor slab
5   Door mat
6   Tubular steel 20/40/3 mm
7   Toughened plate glass

Portal der Heilig-Geist-Kirche in Emmerich. Zweiflügelige Tür (Durchgangsflügel rechts) in Leichtmetallguß. Gesamtmaß etwa 3,00 × 3,00 m. In dem vertieften Mittelfeld sitzt eine als Schloß dienende Rosette. Sandguß; die Rosette wurde nach einem Holzmodell eingeformt. Anschlag mit Zapfenbändern und Bodentürschließer an Stahlprofil-Konstruktion.

Bildhauer Franz-Rudolf Knubel, Essen
Architekt Dieter G. Baumewerd, Münster/Westf.

Portal of the Church of the Holy Ghost, Emmerich. Double-leaf door (narrow swing leaf right) in cast light metal. Overall dimensions approx. 3.00 × 3.00 m. A rosette in the recessed centre bay serves as a lock. The rosette was sand cast, moulded on a wood pattern. Stile with mortise hinges and floor closer shutting on to steel profiled frame.

Kath. Gemeindezentrum Bernhausen. Die Türen sind aus 10 mm dicken Aluminiumgußplatten als räumliche Struktur zusammengeschweißt. Die Erstarrungsfläche mit der unregelmäßigen Gußhaut bildet die Außenseite. Anschlag mit Zapfenbändern und Bodentürschließer. Windfangkonstruktion aus Stahlprofilen und Gußdrahtglas. Stahlteile anthrazitgrau gestrichen.

Architekt Dr.-Ing. Reinhard Gieselmann, Wien

R. Cath. Church Hall, Bernhausen. The doors are of 10 mm thick, cast aluminium plates as a space structure. The exterior is formed by the rigid surface with the uneven casting skin. Hanging stile with mortise hinges and floor closer. Vestibule door of steel sections and wired rolled glass. Steel components painted anthracite-grey.

Grundriß 1:50, Detail 1:2

1 Aluminiumguß 10 mm
2 2 L 45/30/5 mm, punktweise verschweißt
3 Stahlblech 2 mm
4 Gußdrahtglas in Neoprenedichtung

Ground plan 1:50, detail 1:2

1 Aluminium casting, 10 mm
2 2 L 45/30/5 mm, point-welded
3 2 mm steel sheet
4 Wire-reinforced, rolled glass in neoprene sealing gasket

Diese Aluminiumtür 0,70 × 2,00 m, 15 mm dick, wurde als offener Sandguß aus einer seewasserfesten Alu-Legierung hergestellt. Sie ist als Schiebetür konstruiert und hängt an Rollen. Außerdem seitlich unten eine Führungsrolle. Auf einer Seite hat die Tür einen Schiebegriff in Form einer Hand.

Entwurf Glas + Form, Florian Lechner, Neubeuern

This aluminium door, 0.70 × 2.20 m, 15 mm thick, was produced as an open sand casting from a seawater-resistant, aluminium alloy. It is designed as a sliding door and is hung on rollers. There is also a bottom guide at the side. On one side the door has a push-plate in the form of a hand.

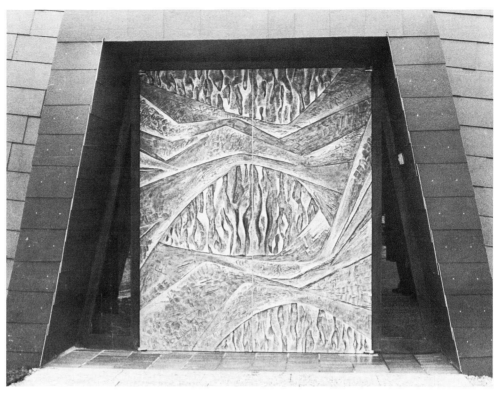

Ev. Auferstehungskirche in Dünsbach. Jeder Flügel trägt innen und außen eine etwa 1 cm starke Platte aus Aluminiumguß, die in Grautönen patiniert wurde. (Sandguß nach Styropor-Modell). In das Relief der Platte sind auch die muschelartigen Türgriffe einbezogen. Flügelmaß 1,00 × 2,20 m. Unterkonstruktion aus Rechteckstahlrohr 60/60/4 mm, feuerverzinkt. Zwischenraum mit Isolierplatten gedämmt. Bodentürschließer und Zapfenbänder. Anschlag an braungestrichenem Blockrahmen. Gummidichtung im Falz.

Bildhauerin Angelika Wetzel, Stuttgart
Architekt Johannes Wetzel, Stuttgart

Protestant Church of the Resurrection, Duensbach. Each wing has a cast aluminium plate approx. 1 cm thick, both inside and outside, anodized in greyish tones. (Sand casting from rigid polystyrene pattern). Shell-type door handles are incorporated in the panel relief. Wing dimension: 1.00 × 2.20 m. Sub-structure of rectangular steel tube 60/60/4 mm, hot-dip galvanized. The intermediary cavity contains thermal insulating slabs. Floor closer and mortise hinges. Door casing brown-painted block frames. Rubber sealing in rebate.

Eingangstüren der kath. Kirche St. Marien in Sindelfingen. Auf einem Rahmen aus Rechteckstahlrohren sind außen Aluguß-Platten, 1,22 × 2,30 m, innen eine Stahlblechplatte aufgeschraubt. Die Griffe sind angegossen.

Architekt Paul Nagler, Sindelfingen

Entrance doors to the R. Cath. Church of St. Mary, Sindelfingen. Cast aluminium plates, 1.22 × 2.30 m, (exterior) and steel sheet panels (interior) are screwed on to the rectangular steel tube framing. The handles are integrally cast.

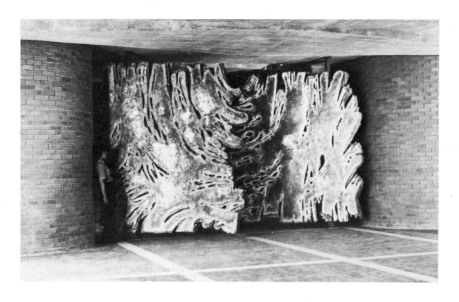

Aussegnungshalle des Friedhofs Joncherolles in Pierrefitte-Villetaneuse. Die zweiflügelige Türanlage ist 5,00 × 2,50 m groß. Die Flügel sind außermittig schwenkbar. Sie haben eine Unterkonstruktion aus Stahlprofilen, die von beiden Seiten mit ausgesägten Messingblechen belegt und dann mit geschmolzenem Zinn überzogen wurden. Das Glitzern des Metalls kontrastiert mit dem Sichtbeton und dem umgebenden Mauerwerk.

Bildhauer Pierre Sabatier, Paris
Architekt R. Auzelle, Paris

Memorial Hall of the Joncherolles Cemetery at Pierrefitte-Villetaneuse. The double-leaf door structure measures 5.00 × 2.50 m. The wings, which are eccentrically pivoting, have a substructure of steel sections with cladding on both sides of sawn brass sheet finished with poured molten tin. The coruscation of the metal is in pleasing contrast to the fair-faced concrete and masonry surround.

Trausaal im Rathaus von Grenoble. Zwei exzentrisch gelagerte schwenkbare Flügel unter-
teilen den Saal entweder in zwei gesonderte
Bereiche, wobei der Raum als Ganzes spürbar
bleibt, oder sie grenzen den Bezirk ein, der für
das Brautpaar bestimmt ist. Die Unterkonstruktion, ein Stahlfachwerk, trägt auf beiden Seiten,
auf einer Unterlage aus Messingblechen, Flächen von aufgeschmolzenem, vielfach durch-
brochenem Zinn. Die Flügel sind 5,20 m breit
und 2,30 m hoch und trotz ihres beträchtlichen
Gewichtes leicht schwenkbar.

Bildhauer Pierre Sabatier, Paris
Architekt Maurice Novarina, Paris

Registry Office in the Town Hall, Grenoble.
Two eccentrically supported, pivoting leaves
divide the hall into two separate areas of
activity while preserving the overall unity of
the area, or they partition off the bridal ceremonial area. The steel lattice sub-structure
has a brass sheet backing supporting an irre-
gular filigree of molten tin with extensive
openwork. The wings are 5.20 m wide and
2.30 m high, and, in spite of their massive
weight, are easily pivoted.

Empfangshalle im Rathaus von Grenoble. Wandgestaltung aus getriebenem und patiniertem Messing. Breite 12 m, Höhe 3,30 m. Der Mittelteil, etwa 1,80 m breit, ist an einer exzentrisch gestellten Achse schwenkbar. Dieser als Tür dienende Teil trägt auf beiden Seiten ein Messingrelief und wiegt ca. 400 kg. Das Relief korrespondiert formal mit einem Wandbehang an der gegenüberliegenden Saalwand. Es ist stellenweise für die Zu- und Abluftöffnung der Klimaanlage durchbrochen.

Bildhauer Pierre Sabatier, Paris
Architekt Maurice Novarina, Paris

Reception Hall, Town Hall, Grenoble. Decorative wall in embossed and anodized brass. Width 12 m, height 3.30 m. The centre panel, approx. 1.80 m wide, is pivoted on an eccentric hinge and acts as a door. It has a brass relief on each side and weighs approx. 400 kg. The relief harmonizes with a mural on the opposite wall of the Hall. It is perforated at various points by air conditioning intake and outlet apertures.

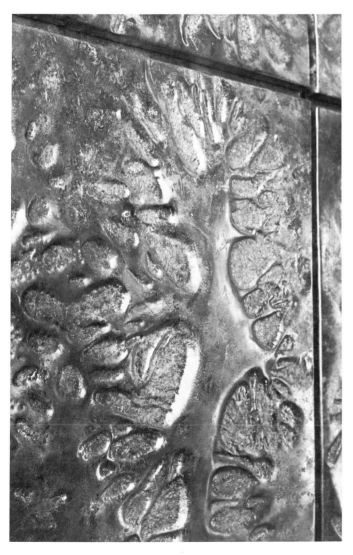

Kathedrale von Nanterre. Das Portal ist 6,40 × 13,20 m groß, aus Messing getrieben und mit Blei und Zinn beschmolzen. Sein Motiv ist der brennende Dornbusch. Die beiden untersten Felder bilden die Durchgangsflügel. Sie sind auf der Innenseite ebenso gearbeitet wie außen.

Bildhauer Pierre Sabatier, Paris

Cathedral of Nanterre. The portal, measuring 6.40 × 13.20 m, is of chased brass with a poured finish of molten lead and tin. The two lower bays form the access door. The surface finish is the same on both interior and exterior.

Departement-Verwaltung Val de Marne, Creteil/Frankreich. Die Schiebewände in der Empfangshalle sind 3,50 m hoch, aus Messing getrieben und patiniert.
Bildhauer Pierre Sabatier, Paris
Architekt D. Badani, Paris

Administrative Headquarters of the Department of Val de Marne, Creteil/France. The sliding walls in the reception hall are 3.50 m high, of embossed and anodized brass.

Festsaal im Bezirkshaus des 9. Arrondissements, Paris. Der Eiserne Vorhang ist aus Messing, getrieben und patiniert. Er wird mechanisch bewegt. Maße 9,00 × 3,50 m.
Bildhauer Pierre Sabatier, Paris
Architekt Oberdoerfer, Paris

Banqueting Chamber in the Metropolitan District Headquarters of the 9th Arrondissement, Paris. The "Iron Curtain" is of embossed and anodized brass, mechanically operated. Dimensions 9.00 × 3.50 m.

Kath. Kirche St. Matthias, Fürstenried. Die Türblätter, 2,50 × 1,30 m groß, sind aus Sperrholz und mit 2 mm dickem, dunkel patiniertem Messingblech bekleidet. Türbänder, Griffe und Zarge aus demselben Material.

Entwurf und Ausführung Manfred und German Bergmeister, Ebersberg
Architekt Alexander Frhr. von Branca, München

R. Cath. Church of St. Matthew, Fuerstenried. The door leaves, 2.50 × 1.30 m, are of plywood with a 2 mm thick cladding of dark, anodized brass sheet. Door hinges, handles and casing are all of the same material.

Eingangstür der kath. Kirche St. Hildegard in München. Die zweiflügelige Tür, 2,70 × 3,60 m groß, hat eine Unterkonstruktion aus Stahlprofilen und ist mit 6 mm starkem Bronzeblech beschlagen. Die Schweißnähte stehen kräftig auf der sonst unbehandelten Fläche. Die Türgriffe sind als Umkantung des Beschlagbleches aufgefaßt.

Entwurf und Ausführung Manfred und German Bergmeister, Ebersberg

Entrance door to R. Cath. Church of St. Hildegard, Munich. The double-leaf door, 2.70 × 3.60 m in size, has a steel sectional base structure with all fittings of 6 mm thick bronze sheet. The seam welds stand out boldly against the otherwise untreated surface. The door handles are designed as a welt of the door trim sheet.

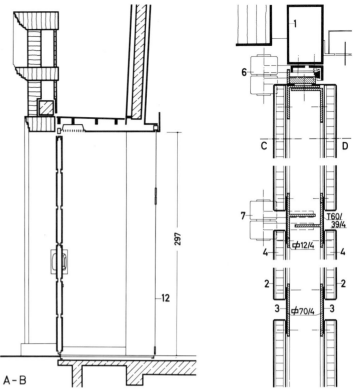

A – B

Schnitt und Grundriß 1:50, Details 1:5
Section and ground plan 1:50. Details 1:5

Stadtkirche Jever. Für das südliche Eingangsportal wurde das Portalgewände der abgebrannten Barockkirche verwendet. Verbindung der Messingverkleidung mit den Spanplatten durch angelötete Messinglaschen 20/20/1,5 mm alle 20 bis 30 cm.

Architekt Dieter Oesterlen, Hannover

City Church, Jever. The architrave of the burnt-out Baroque church was employed for the south entrance portal. The brass cladding is attached to the particle boards by means of soldered brass butt straps 20/20/1.5 mm, at 20 to 30 cm intervals.

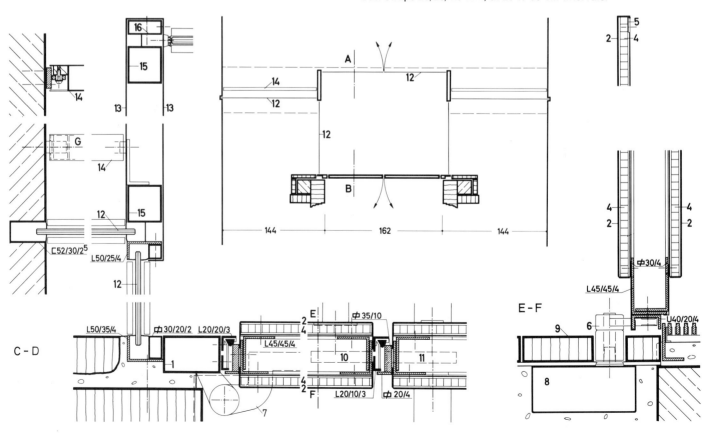

Rathaus in Kehlen. Die zweiflügelige Tür mißt 2,50 × 2,50 m (Gehflügel 1,50 m breit). Das Vollholz-Türblatt ist beidseitig mit 1 mm Kupferblech bekleidet, das unbehandelt blieb und inzwischen dunkle Patina zeigt. Türgriff aus Rotguß. Zargenkonstruktion aus dunkelbraun offenporig gestrichener Kiefer.

Architekt Hans Kley, Rißegg

Town Hall, Kehlen. The double-leaf door measures 2.50 × 2.50 m (swing door 1.50 m wide). The solid wood door leaf is clad on both sides with 1 mm thick copper sheet, left untreated, which has meanwhile acquired a dark patina. Door handle of red bronze. Door casing of pine open-pore paint coating.

◁

1 Stahlrohr 80/50/2,5 mm
2 Messingblech 1,5 mm, brüniert
3 Messingblech 1 mm, brüniert
4 wasserfest verleimtes Sperrholz 16 mm
5 angelötete Messinglasche 20/20/15 mm
6 Zapfenband und Türschiene mit Anschweißauge 40 mm
7 Zwischenband
8 Türschließer Geze Stop einseitig
9 herausnehmbare Steinplatte
10 Panik-Treibriegelverschluß, von innen verschließbar
11 BKS-Hauptschloß, Messing
12 Sekurit-Glas 6–8 mm
13 Stahlblech 1,5 mm, graphit gestrichen
14 Brüstungsstange, Messing brüniert, ⌀ 35 mm
15 Stahlrohr 50/50/2,5 mm
16 Stahlrohr 50/20/2 mm

1 Steel pipe 80/50/2.5 mm
2 1.5 mm burnished brass sheet
3 1 mm burnished brass sheet
4 Waterproof, glued laminated plywood, 16 mm
5 Soldered brass butt straps, 20/20/15 mm
6 Mortise hinge and door rail with welded-on lugs 40 mm
7 Intermediary hinge
8 Door closer, stand-open position 90 to 110°
9 Removable stone slabs
10 Panic bolt with lock, lockable from inside
11 Main cylindrical lock, brass
12 Safety glass, 6–8 mm
13 1.5 mm steel sheet, graphite painted
14 35 mm dia. burnished brass parapet bar
15 Steel tube 50/50/2.5 mm
16 Steel tube 50/50/2 mm

Dreifaltigkeitskirche, Biberach/Riß. Die Eingangstüren sind aus Holz und mit 2 mm Kupferblech beschlagen. Türflügel 2,20 × 1,12 m, Blattdicke 14,5 cm. Gliederung durch etwa 3 cm tiefe Nuten.

Architekten Rainer Zinsmeister und Giselher Scheffler, Stuttgart

Church of the Holy Trinity, Biberach/Riss. The entrance doors are of wood with 2 mm copper sheet furniture. Door wing 2.20 m × 1.12 m, leaf thickness 14.5 cm. Panelling by means of grooves to a depth of approx. 3 cm.

Hauptportal der Zwölf-Apostel-Kirche in Augsburg. Die zweiflügelige Tür mißt 2,50 × 3,00 m. Sie ist mit Kupferblech 62,5 × 50 cm bekleidet. Griffe aus Bronzeguß. Die von den Türbändern nach außen geführten, abgewinkelten Metallstreifen dienen als federnder Türanschlag.

Architekt Dr.-Ing. Clemens Holzmeister, Salzburg

Main portal of the Church of the Twelve Apostles, Augsburg. The double-leaf door measures 2.50 × 3.00 m. It has a cladding of 62.5 × 50 cm copper sheet. Handles of cast bronze. The cranked, metal strips extending outwards from the door hinges act as spring closers.

Schnitt 1:5

1 Stahlhohlprofil
2 Spanplatte 24 mm
3 Kupferblech 1 mm
4 Eiche natur, 22/144 mm

Section 1:5

1 Hollow steel section
2 24 mm particle board panel
3 Copper sheet, 1 mm
4 Natural oak, 22/144 mm

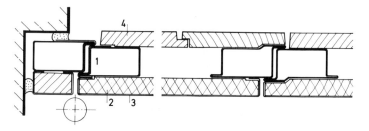

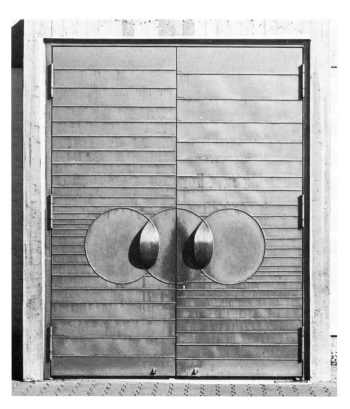

Kath. Kirche in Katzwang. Die zweiflügelige Tür, Gesamtmaß 2,39 × 3,00 m, hat einen tragenden Rahmen aus Stahlhohlprofilen. Außen sind Spanplatten 24 mm aufgesetzt und mit 1 mm Kupferblech bekleidet. Das Blech ist bis in die Innenfälze gezogen und dort verschraubt. Die Nähte der Kupferstreifen sind schutzgas-verschweißt. Türgriffe Bronzeguß. Innere Türbekleidung massive Eichenbretter. Türbänder mit brünierten Messing-Überschubhülsen. Gehflügel mit Bodentürschließer.

Entwurf Hans Rucker, München
Architekt Friedrich F. Haindl, München

R. Cath. Church, Katzwang. The double-leaf door, overall dimensions 2.39 × 3.00 m, has a loadbearing frame of hollow steel sections. 24 mm particle board panels are set on the exterior and clad with 1 mm copper sheet. The sheet is drawn into the internal rebates and screwed down. The copper strips have inert gas-welded seams. Door handles of cast bronze. Interior door cladding of solid oak planking. Door hinges with burnished brass bushings. Swing door with floor closer.

Eingangstüren an einem Zweifamilienhaus. Zargenelement aus Stahlprofilen. Türen mit Kupferblech beschlagen, stark aufgetragene Schweißnähte. Türgriffe aus Schmiedebronze. Das Feld zwischen den Türen trägt die Hausnummer, darunter Klingelknöpfe, Namensschilder und Briefeinwurf.

Entwurf und Ausführung Werkkunst Peters, Stolberg

Entrance doors to a semi-detached house. Door trim of steel profiles. Door fittings of copper sheet with boldly emphasized seam welds. Handles of forged bronze. The narrow bay between the doors bears the house number and underneath has the bell-push, nameplate and letter-box.

Stadtbücherei Wilhelmspalais, Stuttgart. Eingang zum Vortragssaal. Die zweiflügelige Tür ist 2,20 × 2,42 m groß und hat einen tragenden Rahmen aus Rechteckstahlrohr mit einer Sperrholzfüllung. Die Außenseite ist mit 1,5 mm Kupferblech belegt. Die Blechstücke sind dachförmig abgekantet, neben- und übereinander gelegt und miteinander verschweißt. Türgriffe Bronzeguß. Die Innenseiten der Tür sind nußbaumfurniert.

Bildhauer Fritz Melis, Bietigheim-Metterzimmern
Architekt Wilhelm Tiedje, Stuttgart

City Library, Wilhelms Palais, Stuttgart. Entrance to lecture hall. The double-wing door, measuring 2.20 × 2.42 m, has a loadbearing frame of rectangular steel tube with plywood panelling. The exterior is laid with 1.5 mm copper sheet cladding. The sheet units are in canted, "roof"-type pattern, juxtaposed or at right-angles, and welded together. Handles of cast bronze. The door has an interior lining of walnut veneer.

Einfamilienhaus in Kastellaun. Die zweiflügelige Tür hat ein Öffnungsmaß von 1,76 × 2,25 m, Gehflügel 1,00 m breit. Rahmen aus Aluminiumprofilen, Füllung aus Sperrholz, Innenseite mit Edelfurnier. Auf der Außenseite sind 56 mm dicke Holzspanplatten aufgebracht, die in Abstufungen von 8 mm ausgeschnitten sind und die Unterlage für die aus 1,0 mm Kupferblech getriebene Bekleidung bilden. Türgriff als versenkte Mulde getrieben. Das Kupferblech wurde brüniert und gewachst. Türblattdicke insgesamt etwa 12,5 cm.

Entwurf und Ausführung Hermann Gradinger, Mainz

Detached house, Kastellaun. The double-leaf door has an opening of 1.76 × 2.25 m. Swing door 1.00 m wide. Aluminium sectional frame with plywood panelling, interior with decorative veneer. Chipboard panels, 56 mm thick, have been applied to the exterior, cut out in 8 mm step formation to form the base for the 1.0 mm chased, copper sheet cladding. Door pull in the form of a recessed, chased trough. The copper sheet was burnished and waxed. Door leaf thickness altogether approx. 12.5 cm.

Hölzernes Türblatt, mit getriebenem Kupferblech belegt. Zarge Lärchenholz natur. Die drei Blechstücke sind mit Nägeln auf der Unterkonstruktion befestigt. Nähte überfälzt. Griff Bronzeguß.

Bildhauer Franz Gutmann, Münstertal

Wooden door leaf, covered with chased, copper sheet. Door casing natural larch wood. The three sheet components are nailed to the sub-base. Welted seams. Handle in cast bronze.

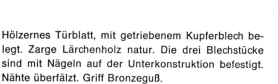

Portal der Marienkirche, Berlin. Die beiden Doppeltüren, Flügelmaß jeweils 0,75 × 4,63 m, sind mit einer aus einem Stück 0,8 mm dickem Kupferblech getriebenen Platte bekleidet, die brüniert und teilweise patiniert wurde. Griffe aus Bronzeguß. Unterkonstruktion Profilstahl, Anschlagzarge aus Rechteckstahlrohr.

Entwurf und Ausführung Achim Kühn, Berlin-Grünau

Portal of the Church of the Virgin Mary, Berlin. The two double doors, with a wing dimension of 0.75 × 4.63 m, are each clad with a single piece of 0.8 mm chased copper sheet burnished and partly anodized. Handle of cast bronze. Sub-structure of sectional steel, door jambs of rectangular steel tube.

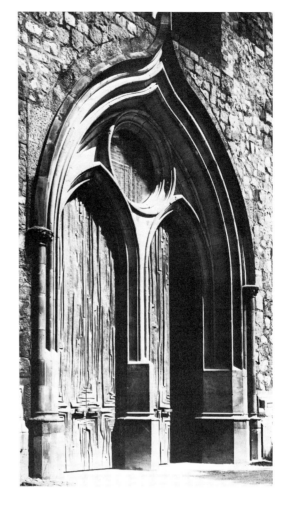

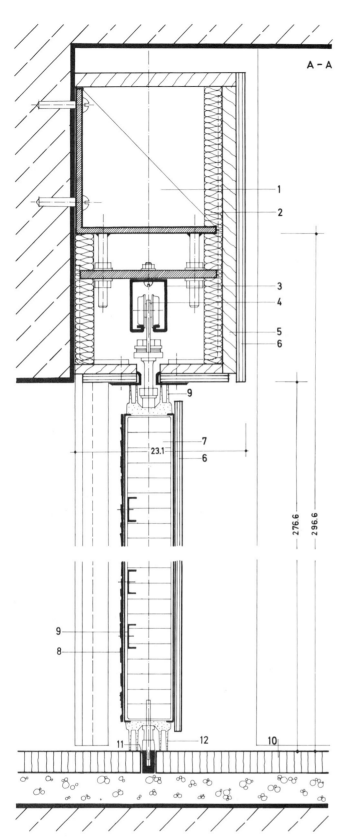

A – A

23.1

276.6 296.6

Theodor-Heuss-Gymnasium, Esslingen. Die schalldichte Schiebewand zwischen Eingangshalle und Aula trägt auf der Seite der Halle ein Flachrelief aus Zinkplatten.

Entwurf Brigitte Beyer, Esslingen
Architekten Karst + Kimmig, Stuttgart

Theodor Heuss Grammar School, Esslingen. The acoustic, soundproof wall between the entrance and assembly hall has a bas-relief of zinc sheets.

1 Aufhängung Winkelprofil 200/200/10 mm
2 Isolierung 25 mm
3 Laufschiene
4 je Tafel 2 Aufhängungen
5 Spanplatte 19 mm
6 Furnierplatte 12 mm, nußbaumfurniert
7 Wandelement 1,40 × 2,76 m, 7 cm dick
8 Zinkauflage, 2–5 mm dick, aufgeschraubt
9 U-Schienen zur Befestigung der Zinkauflage
10 Marmorplatten, Jura gelb
11 Führungsschiene, Messing
12 Dichtungsprofil
13 verlängerter Bedienungshebel
14 Verriegelung
15 Schleifgummi
16 Gummidichtung
17 Türgriff der Durchgangstür, versenkt

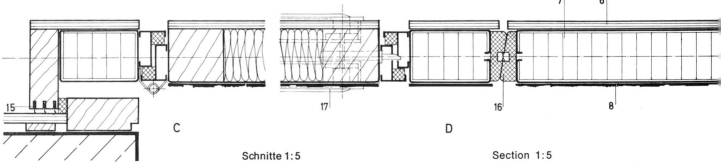

C   D

Schnitte 1:5   Section 1:5

1 Suspension angle bar
  200/200/10 mm
2 Insulation, 25 mm
3 Runners
4 2 suspension units per panel
5 Particle board, 19 mm
6 Veneer panel, 12 mm, walnut
  veneered
7 Wall unit, 1.40 × 2.76 m, 7 cm
  thick
8 Zinc overlay, 2–5 mm thick,
  screwed on

B-B

Ansicht und Grundriß 1:60

Elevation and ground plan 1:60

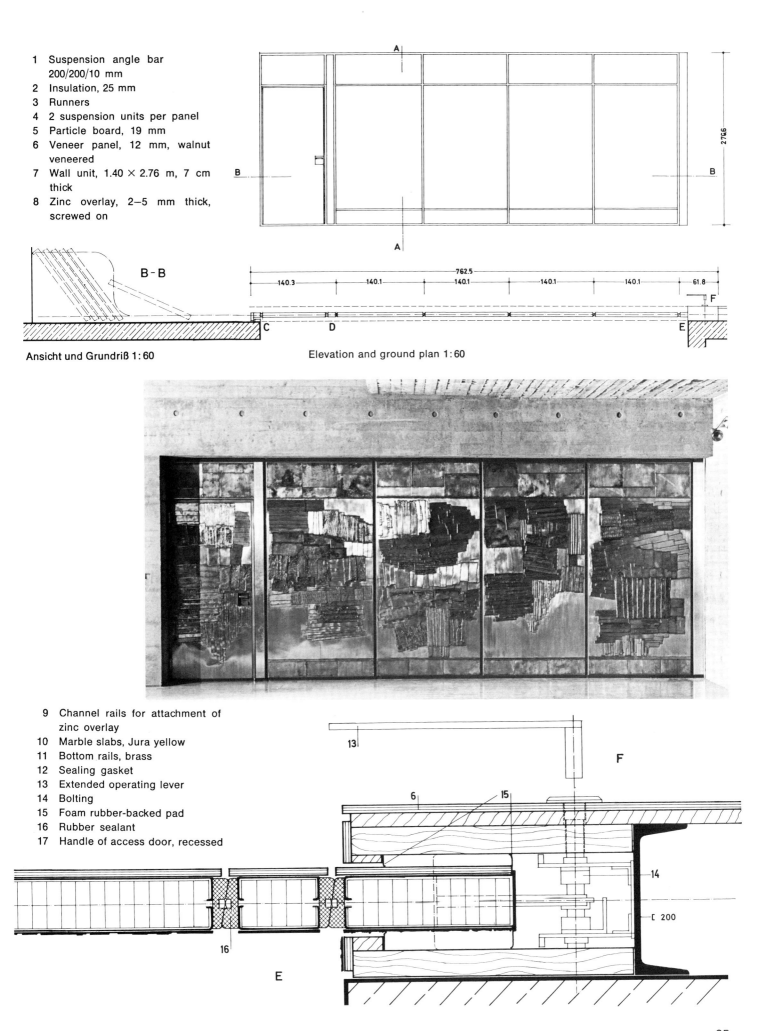

9 Channel rails for attachment of
  zinc overlay
10 Marble slabs, Jura yellow
11 Bottom rails, brass
12 Sealing gasket
13 Extended operating lever
14 Bolting
15 Foam rubber-backed pad
16 Rubber sealant
17 Handle of access door, recessed

35

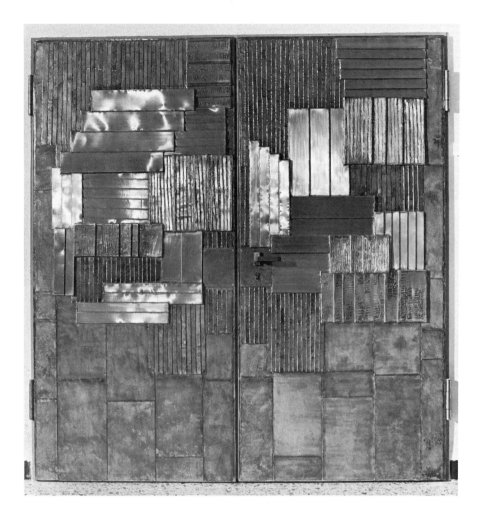

Kreiskrankenhaus Schorndorf. Tür von der Eingangshalle in die Krankenhauskapelle. Die hölzernen Türblätter, je 1,00 × 2,5 m groß, sind auf beiden Seiten mit einem Relief aus Zinkplatten bekleidet, das sich aus Streifen mit verschiedener Struktur und Oberflächenbehandlung (z. T. sandgestrahlt) zusammensetzt. Nähte und Verbindungen gelötet.

Bildhauerin Brigitte Beyer, Esslingen
Architekt Hermann Längerer, Stuttgart

District hospital, Schorndorf. Door from the entrance foyer to the hospital chapel. The wooden door leaves, each 1.00 × 2.50 m in size, are clad on both sides with a relief composed of zinc sheet strips of varying textures and surface finishes (e. g. sand blasted). Seams and connections soldered.

Kath. Kirche St. Johannes, Karlsruhe-Durlach. Das Hauptportal, 2,50 × 2,50 m groß, ist aus massiven, 6 cm dicken Eichenbohlen hergestellt und beiderseits mit getriebenen Bleiplatten bekleidet. Die Tür ist wie ein Wendeflügel um ihre Mittelachse drehbar.

Bildhauer Josef H. Weber, Grötzingen in Zusammenarbeit mit Guido Messer
Architekt Rainer Disse, Karlsruhe

R. Cath. Church of St. John, Karlsruhe-Durlach. The main portal, 2.50 × 2.50 m in size, is made of solid oak boards, 6 cm thick, with chased, lead sheet cladding on both sides. The door revolves on its centre axis like a vertically pivoted door.

Landessparkasse Stuttgart. Die zweiflügelige Tür ist ca. 2,55 × 2,15 m groß und hat einen Rahmen aus Rechteckstahlrohr mit Holzfüllung. Jeder Flügel ist mit drei getriebenen Aluminiumblechplatten bekleidet, Dicke 1,5 mm. Dabei steht das mittlere Feld jeweils 4 cm vor den Feldern oben und unten. Das Aluminium wurde patiniert und farblos lackiert. Die Innenflächen sind mit glattem Aluminiumblech bekleidet.

Bildhauer Hannes Neuner, Stuttgart
Architekt Ludwig Schweizer, Stuttgart

Regional Savings Bank, Stuttgart. The double-wing door is approx. 2.55 × 2.15 m in size and has a frame of rectangular tubular steel with wood panelling. Each wing has a cladding of three chased, aluminium sheet panels, thickness 1.5 mm. The middle bay projects 4 cm respectively beyond the upper and lower bays. The aluminium was anodized and coated with transparent varnish. The interior surfaces have smooth, aluminium sheet cladding.

Eingangsgitter aus Leichtmetall für ein Wohnhaus. Gesamtmaß 2,20 × 2,40 m. Es überdeckt den dahinterliegenden Eingang, eine Metall-Glas-Konstruktion mit Betonsturz. Die Eingangstür rechts mißt 0,80 × 2,10 m. Ober- und Untergurt des Gitters bestehen aus einem Aluminium-Rechteckrohr 60/40/3 mm. Daran sind Aluminium-Blechstreifen von 150/6 bis 60/6 mm geschweißt, im Wechsel davor und dahinter. Die Streifen sind durch Rechtecke verbunden, die jeweils aus zwei benachbarten Blechen ausgehauen, gegeneinander gerückt und verschweißt sind. Das Aluminium wurde gebürstet, schwarz eingefärbt und mit Stahlwolle abgerieben.

Entwurf und Ausführung Hermann Gradinger, Mainz

Entrance grille of light metal for a detached house. Overall dimensions 2.20 × 2.40 m. The grille covers the entrance door behind, of metal-glass construction, with concrete lintol. The entrance door, right, measures 0.80 × 2.10 m. The upper and lower flanges of the grille consist of aluminium tubes of rectangular section 60/40/3 mm. Sheet aluminium strips are welded onto these alternately in front and behind. The strips are connected by rectangles cut out from two adjacent sheets, folded back against each other and welded together. The aluminium was satinized, stained black and rubbed down with steel wool.

Zweiflügelige Tür an der Remshalle in Essingen. Rahmen-konstruktion aus 80 mm Kiefernholz, beidseitig mit 0,5 mm Edelstahlblech beschlagen, das kalt getrieben wurde. Die Bleche sind am Rand abgekantet und im Falz der Holztüren verschraubt. Halbkreisförmige Türgriffe aus Edelstahl ⌀ 40 cm. Anschlag an Holzrahmen mit dreiteiligen Türbändern, Edelstahl. Bodentürschließer mit Schwinghebel.

Architekten Rothmaier + Tröster, Ellwangen/Jagst
Ausführung Emil Schneider, Essingen

Double-leaf door at the Rems Hall, Essingen. Frame construction of 80 mm pine, with 0.5 mm stainless steel, cold-worked fittings on each side. The sheets are chamfered at the edges and screwed into the rebate of the wooden doors. Semi-circular door handles of stainless steel, dia. 40 cm. Hung on a wooden frame with 3-part hinges in stainless steel. Floor closer with pivoting arm.

Stadthalle Sindelfingen. Die Türflügel messen 1,08 × 2,20 m, besitzen eine Rahmenkonstruktion aus Rechteckstahl-rohr und sind von beiden Seiten mit Aluminiumblech bekleidet. Für die Treibar-beiten an der Außenseite sind weiche Aluminium-Tafeln von 1,5 mm Dicke verwendet. Nach den vom Bildhauer darauf vorgezeichneten Linien wurde das Blech getrieben. Dadurch und durch das anschließende Planieren wurden die Tafeln steif und hart. Die fertigen Bleche natur eloxiert. Türgriffe Aluminiumguß.

Bildhauer Emil Cimiotti
Ausführung Manfred Kühner, Stuttgart

City Hall, Sindelfingen. The door wings, measuring 1.08 × 2.20 m, have rectangular tubular steel framing with aluminium sheet cladding on each side. Soft aluminium panels. 1.5 mm thick, were employed for the elaborate working of the external surface. The sheet was chased according to lines previously marked out by the sculptor. This procedure and subsequent planishing caused the panels to become stiff and rigid. The finished sheets were anodized in a natural colour. Door handles of cast aluminium.

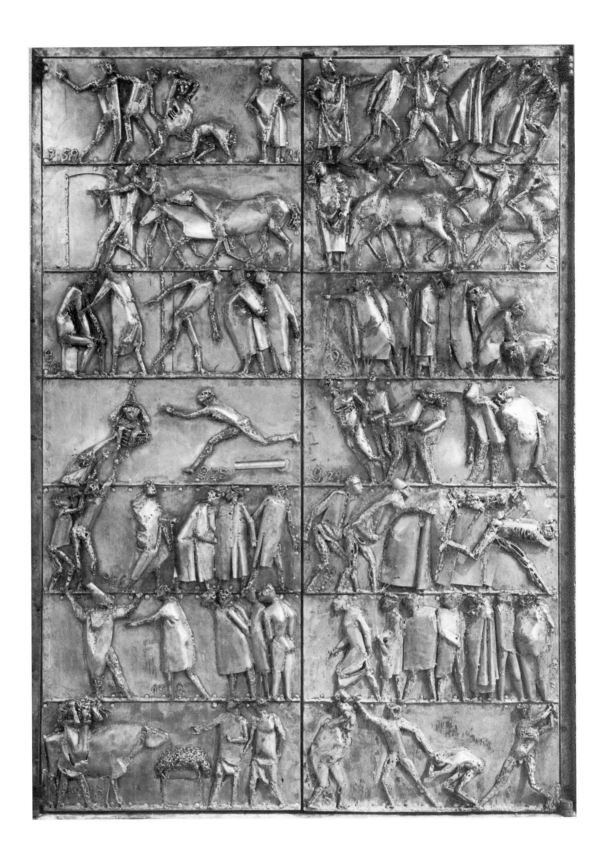

St. Paulus Kirche, Salzgitter-Lebenstedt. Jedes Türblatt ist 0,75 × 2,20 m groß und aus sieben Feldern
zusammengesetzt, die Szenen aus der Apostelge-
schichte darstellen. Die Figuren sind aus Edelstahl
geschmiedet und elektrisch aufgeschweißt. Auch die
einzelnen Felder, 73 × 31 cm, sind durch Elektro-
schweißen mit der stabilen Rahmenkonstruktion verbunden.

Bildhauer Karl Henning Seemann, Löchgau

St. Paul's Church, Salzgitter-Lebenstedt. Each door
leaf is 0.75 × 2.20 m in size and is composed of
7 bays depicting scenes from the lives of the Apostles. The figures are of wrought steel, electro-welded.
The individual panels, 73 × 31 cm, are also attached
to the solid frame by electro-welding.

Ev. Kirche in Mülheim-Heissen. Eingangsportal mit Edelstahl bekleidet. Die aufgesetzten Figuren in Bronzeguß zeigen Christus, der über den Wassern predigt.

Bildhauer Max Kratz, Düsseldorf

Prot. Church at Muelheim-Heissen. Entrance portal with stainless steel cladding. The figures superimposed in cast bronze represent Christ's Sermon over the Waters.

Eingangstüren an der Stadthalle in Karl-Marx-Stadt. Die mit Zapfenbändern angeschlagenen Türflügel messen jeweils 1,00 × 2,30 m. Sie sind mit 2 mm Edelstahlblech bekleidet, auf das geschmiedete und grau-blau lasierte Profile aus Baustahl 25/12 mm aufgesetzt sind. Türgriffe Edelstahl 15 mm.

Entwurf Achim Kühn, Berlin-Grünau

Entrance doors to the City Hall, Karl-Marx-City. The door leaves, having hanging stiles with mortise hinges, each measure 1.00 × 2.30 m. They have 2 mm stainless steel sheet cladding on which are superimposed wrought and greyish-blue, structural steel sections 25/12 mm with transparent glazing. Door handles of 15 mm stainless steel.

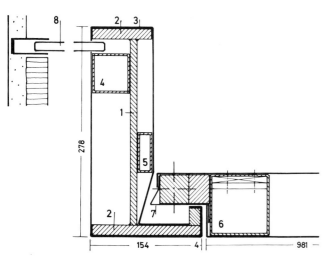

Schnitt 1:5	Section 1:5
1 Stahl 10 mm	1 Steel, 10 mm
2 Stahl 15 mm	2 Steel, 15 mm
3 Edelstahlblech 2 mm	3 Stainless steel sheet, 2 mm
4 Stahlrohr 50/50/2 mm	4 Steel tube, 50/50/2 mm
5 Stahlrohr 50/20/2 mm	5 Steel tube, 50/20/2 mm
6 Stahlrohr 80/80/2 mm	6 Steel tube, 80/80/2 mm
7 Edelstahlblech 1 mm	7 Stainless steel sheet, 1 mm
8 Drahtfadenverbund-glas 8 mm	8 Wire-thread reinforced, laminated safety glass, 8 mm

Eingangstüren der Deutschen Bank, Köln. Die Flügel sind 1,98 × 2,33 m groß, haben eine Innenkonstruktion aus Stahlprofilen und sind auf beiden Seiten mit 2 mm Edelstahlblech bekleidet. Auf das geschliffene Blech von Tür und Rahmen sind 8 mm dicke hochglanzpolierte Edelstahlstücke gelegt. Anschlag an einer freistehenden im Boden verankerten Zarge mit kugelgelagerten Zapfenbändern.

Bildhauer Max Kratz, Düsseldorf
Bauabteilung der Deutschen Bank (Architekt Blume)

Entrance doors to Deutsche Bank, Cologne. The wings, dimensions 1.98 × 2.33 m, have an inner core system of steel sections and 2 mm stainless steel cladding on both sides. The smooth-ground sheet surface of the door and frame is set with highly polished, stainless steel "stones", roughly rectangular. Door hung on a free-standing casing with floor anchorage and mortise hinges on ball-bearings.

Zweiflügelige Eingangstür an einem Wohnhaus. In den feststehenden Flügel ist ein röhrenförmiger Körper ⌀ 400 mm eingesetzt, der den Briefkasten (Einwurfklappe in der Mitte), die Sprechanlage (oben) sowie Namenszug und Klingelknopf enthält. Die Tür ist vollflächig mit natur eloxiertem Leichtmetallblech bekleidet.

Architekten W. Döring, E. Syffus, H. Keune, Düsseldorf

Double-leaf entrance door to a detached house. A tubular component, 400 mm in dia., is installed in the fixed leaf to accommodate the letter-box (letter-plate in centre) intercom (top), nameplate and door-bell. The door is flush with natural anodized, light metal sheet cladding.

Gemeindezentrum Ilvesheim. Die Tür links führt zum Gemeindesaal, die zweiflügelige Tür zur Kirche. Sie mißt 2,65 × 2,90 m. Die Flügel haben eine Unterkonstruktion aus Profilstahl und sind vollflächig mit rostfreiem Stahlblech bekleidet, das umgekantet und im Falz verschraubt ist. Griffe aus Edelstahl ⌀ 25 mm. Türzarge Stahl, dunkel lackiert.

Architekt Helmut Striffler, Mannheim-Lindenhof

Church hall, Ilvesheim. The door (left) leads to the community hall, the double-leaf door to the church. Dimensions 2.65 × 2.90 m. The wings have a substructure of sectional steel and are flush with stainless steel cladding which is folded back and screwed into the rebate. Handle of stainless steel, 25 mm in dia. Door trim of steel with dark paint coating.

Eingang eines Einfamilienhauses. Haustür mit geschliffenem Edelstahl bekleidet. Das Feld daneben ist mit einer shed-ähnlichen Konstruktion aus Edelstahl geschlossen, Scheiben aus Gußglas.

Entrance to a detached house. Front door with polished, stainless steel cladding. The side bay is closed with a ridged, "shed-type" system of stainless steel, cast glass panes.

Trauerhalle Friedhof Frankfurt-Westhausen. Die zweiflügelige Schiebetür hat ein Durchgangsmaß von 3,00 × 3,20 m. Sie ist beidseitig mit Aluminium-Lamellen bekleidet.

Architekt Günter Bock, Frankfurt/M.

Funeral hall, Cemetery at Frankfurt-Westhausen. The double-leaf sliding door has an opening dimension of 3.00 × 3.20 m. Aluminium slat cladding on both sides.

Schnitte 1:5

1 Stahlblech gestrichen, 2 mm
2 Aluminium-Lamellenprofil
3 Flachstahl 60/9 mm
4 Stahlrohr 45/45/2 mm (tragender Rahmen)
5 Hakenriegel-Schloß
6 Neoprene-Dichtung

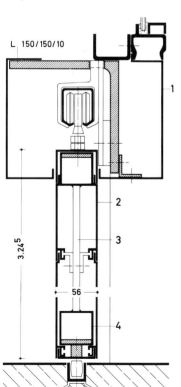

Sections 1:5

1 Painted 2 mm steel sheet
2 Aluminium slat section
3 Flat rolled steel sheet, 60/9 mm
4 Tubular steel 45/45/2 mm (loadbearing frame)
5 Hook-belt lock
6 Neoprene weather sealing

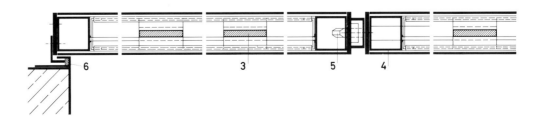

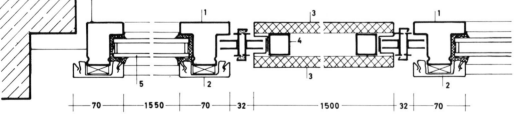

Schnitt 1:5
Section 1:5

1 Profilrohr Stahl
2 Edelstahlblech auf Klemmprofil
3 Edelstahlblech 1,25 mm, abgekantet, an den Ecken verschweißt
  und auf Trägerplatte geklebt
4 Vierkantstahlrohr 30/30/3 mm
5 Zweischeibenisolierglas in Neoprene-Dichtungsprofil

1 Steel tubular section
2 Stainless sheet on clamp section
3 Stainless steel sheet, chamfered and edge-welded and glued
  on to a backing plate
4 Square steel tube 30/30/3 mm
5 Two-piece, laminated insulating glass in neoprene gasket

Ateliergebäude in Hagen/Westfalen. Die Haustür ist wie die Fassade mit Edelstahl bekleidet. Waagrechter Fries 36 cm breit, mit Edelholzfurnier, Türgriff und Briefeinwurf Edelstahl. Türflügel 1,00 × 2,55 m, Seitenteil 0,50 m breit.

Architekt Hans Wenig, Hagen

Studio building in Hagen, Westphalia. The front door like the façade has stainless steel cladding. Horizontal frieze 36 cm wide, with decorative veneer, door handle and letter-plate in stainless steel. Door leaf, 1.00 × 2.55 m, side bay 0.50 m wide.

Eingangstür, als Serientür angefertigt. Das Füllungsblech aus Edelstahl natur ist mit 18 mm Polyurethanschaum hinterlegt, Innenfläche farbige PVC-Beschichtung. Türrahmen und Anschlag aus mit Kunststoff beschichtetem Leichtmetall. Innenliegende Zapfenbänder, Falzdichtung durch Neoprene-Profile.

Entwurf Otto H. Hajek, Stuttgart
Hersteller Oskar D. Biffar K.G., Edenkoben

Entrance door, serially produced. The panel is of natural-coloured, stainless steel with 18 mm polyurethane foam backing and an interior coating of coloured PVC. Door casing and side jamb of plastic-coated light metal. Rebated mortise hinges, rebate sealing with neoprene gasket.

Wohnhaus in Kastellaun. Die Haustür hat einen Aluminiumrahmen und ist innen mit Holz, außen mit 4 mm Aluminiumblech bekleidet. Die drei Platten sind ringsum 15 mm aufgekantet und verschweißt. Das Aluminium wurde gebürstet, schwarz eingefärbt und aluchromiert. Die Gitterfelder sind aus Flachstahl 40/10 und 30/8 mm geschmiedet. Ober- und Untergurt 50/10 mm. Die Gitter können geöffnet werden. Sie sind feuerverzinkt und mit Graphitfarbe gestrichen.

Entwurf und Ausführung Hermann Gradinger, Mainz

Detached house, Kastellaun. The front entrance is aluminium-framed with interior wood cladding and 4 mm aluminium sheet externally. The three panels have a 15 mm raised edge moulding with welded jointing. The grille bays are of wrought, flat bar steel 40/10 and 30/8 mm. Upper and lower flanges 50/10 mm. The grilles are openable. They are hot-dip galvanized and coated with graphite paint.

45

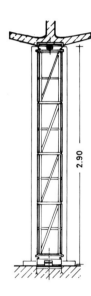

Schnitte 1:50
Sections 1:50

Kapelle Notre Dame du Haut in Ronchamps. Das Hauptportal ist 3,05 × 2,90 m groß und 0,33 m dick. Unterkonstruktion aus Stahlprofilen. Das Türblatt ist auf Kugellagern um seine Mittelachse drehbar und schlägt seitlich in ausgerundete Gußprofile. Innen- und Außenfläche sind mit je acht Blechtafeln 1,35 × 0,66 m belegt, die in lebhaften Farben emailliert sind. Auf der Innenseite ist ein in Bronze gegossener Griff eingelassen.

Architekt Le Corbusier †

Chapel of Notre Dame du Haut, Ronchamps. The main portal dimensions are 3.05 × 2.90 m × 0.33 m thick. Sub-structure of steel sections. The door leaf revolves on ball-bearings on its centre axis and has side jambs rounded, cast sections. The interior and exterior surfaces are each covered with eight metal sheet panels, enamelled in lively colours. A cast bronze hand grip is recessed on the inside.

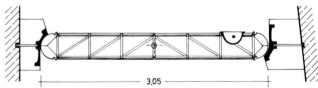

Baden State Theatre, Karlsruhe, Small House. Door between foyer and auditorium. The swing door, right, 1.75 × 2.75 m in dimensions, is part of a wall unit of 4.00 × 3.70 m. The square bar steel framing has 2.5 mm steel sheet cladding on both sides. Intermediary layer of 70 mm mineral wool. Side jambs and stiles with neoprene sealing, above and below automatic door sealant. On the door leaves on each side 3 coloured enamel panels — in green, white and black — are attached respectively (top and bottom clamp sections, at the side screwed to steel angle bars 25/25/3 mm). The fixed panel (left) is similarly faced. Door handle, 50 mm in dia., covered in leather. On the inside panic bolt with pivoted lever; door stay. ▷

Ausbildungszentrum der Deutschen Bundespost, Braunschweig. Zweiflügelige Tür zwischen Pausenhalle und Großem Saal. Die beiden Türblätter, 0,91 × 2,17 m, sind aus 40 mm Tischlerplatten, auf die natur eloxiertes Aluminiumblech aufgeschraubt wurde. Darauf sind die rot, weiß und schwarz emaillierten Stahlbleche ebenfalls aufgeschraubt.
Maler Gerd Winner, München
Architekt Wolf-Georg Castorf, OPD Braunschweig und E. Lion

Training centre of the Federal German Post Office, Braunschweig. Double-leaf door between the lounge and the Main Hall. The two door-leaves, 0.91 × 2.17 m, are of 40 mm coreboard panels on to which are screwed natural anodized, aluminium sheet. The red, white and black enamelled sheet panels are likewise screwed on to these.

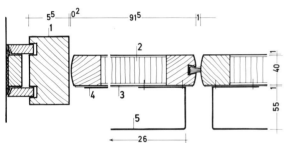

Schnitt 1:5	Section 1:5
1 Blendrahmen 55/92 mm	1 Frame surround 55/92 mm
2 Tischlerplatte 40 mm	2 Coreboard panel, 40 mm
3 Alublech 1 mm	3 Aluminium sheet, 1 mm
4 Stahlblech emailliert 1,5 mm	4 Enamelled steel sheet, 1.5 mm
5 Türgriff Stahlblech emailliert	5 Enamelled steel sheet door push plate

Badisches Staatstheater Karlsruhe, Kleines Haus. Tür zwischen Foyer und Zuschauerraum. Der Gehflügel, rechts, 1,75 × 2,75 m groß, steht in einem Wandelement von 4,00 × 3,70 m. Er hat einen beidseits mit 2,5 mm Stahlblech bekleideten Rahmen aus Vierkantrohren. Zwischenlage 70 mm Mineralwolle. Senkrechte Anschläge mit Neoprene-Dichtung, oben und unten automatische Türabdichter Stadi. Auf dem Türblatt sind auf beiden Seiten je 3 farbig emaillierte Blechtafeln — grün, weiß und schwarz — befestigt (oben und unten Klommprofile, seitlich an Stahlwinkeln 25/25/3 mm geschraubt). Die feststehende Fläche links ist in gleicher Weise aufgedoppelt. Griffstange ⌀ 50 mm mit Leder bezogen. Auf der Innenseite Panikschloß mit Schwenkhebel; Türfeststeller.
Architekt Helmut Bätzner, Karlsruhe

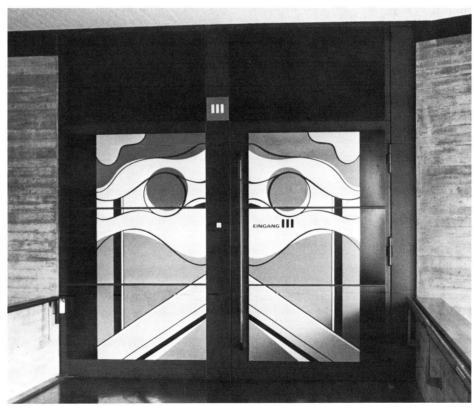

Kath. Kirche St. Marien, Aalen. Tür zur Sakristei. Farbe und Konstruktion wie Seite 49.

Architekt Wilfried Beck-Erlang, Stuttgart

R. Cath. Church of St. Mary, Aalen. Door to sacristy. Colour and design as on page 49.

Kath. Kirche in Kuchen. Das zweiflügelige Hauptportal ist 2,13 × 2,35 m groß. Unterkonstruktion aus Alurohren, belegt mit Leichtmetallblechen, die zur Schloßseite abgestuft in Erscheinung treten und in verschiedenen Blautönen lackiert sind. Hauptflächen geschliffen, gebürstet und natur eloxiert. Anschlagrahmen Leichtmetallprofile, Zapfenbänder, Bodentürschließer.

Bildhauerin Gerlinde Beck, Mühlacker-Großglattbach Architekten B. Perlia, H. W. Schliebitz, J. Schwarz, Stuttgart

R. Cath. Church at Kuchen. The double-leaf main portal measures 2.13 × 2.35 m. Sub-structure of aluminium tubes, covered with light metal sheets which are graduated on the lock side and are painted in different shades of blue. Main surfaces are ground, satinized and natural anodized. Frame jambs light metal sections, mortise hinges, door closers.

Kath. Kirche St. Marien, Aalen. Zweiflügelige Eingangstür, Flügelgröße 1,20 × 2,80 m, Seitenportal 1,50 × 2,40 m. Die Türflügel sind 14 cm dick und auf beiden Seiten mit 1,5 mm Edelstahlblech bekleidet. Die rote Lackierung der Unterkonstruktion tritt auch an den Kanten und im Türfalz in Erscheinung. Die Flügel sind mit Zapfenbändern an einem Rahmen aus dunkelgrau gestrichenen Rechteckstahlrohren angeschlagen.

Bildhauerin Gerlinde Beck, Mühlacker-Großglattbach
Architekt Wilfried Beck-Erlang, Stuttgart

R. Cath. Church of St. Mary, Aalen. Double-leaf entrance door, wing dimensions 1.20 × 2.80 m, side portal 1.50 × 2.40 m. The door wings are 14 cm thick with 1.5 mm stainless steel cladding on each side. The red painting of the sub-structure also appears at the edges and in the door rebate. The door is hung on mortise hinges and the wing stile closes on to a jamb of rectangular steel tubing painted dark grey.

Zweiflügeliger Haupteingang der Urologischen Klinik rechts der Isar, München. Unterkonstruktion aus Rechteckstahlrohr, mit emailliertem Blech bekleidet und ausgeschäumt. Auf die Außenflächen sind Auge, Herz und Nieren als flächige Siebdrucke aufgebracht und mit eingebrannt. Flügelmaß etwa 1,00 × 2,40 m.

Entwurf Manfred Mayerle und Andreas Sobeck, München
Neubauamt Klinikum der Technischen Universität München

Double-leaf main doorway into the Urological Clinic, Munich. Sub-structure of rectangular steel tubing, with enamelled sheet cladding and foam backing. The exterior surface has eye, heart and kidney motifs applied in the form of flat screen prints and then stove-enamelled. Wing dimensions approx. 1.00 × 2.40 m.

Kath. Gemeindezentrum, Weil im Schönbuch. Die zweiflügelige Eingangstür mißt 2,00 × 2,00 m. Sie hat Türblätter aus Sperrholz, die mit 2 mm Aluminiumblech bekleidet sind, das farbig einbrennlackiert ist. Sie sind innen in Schwarz, Gelb und Grün gehalten.

Maler D. F. Domes, Langenargen · Architekt M. Fuchs, Tübingen

R. Cath. Church Hall, Weil in Schoenbuch. The double-wing entrance door measures 2.00 × 2.00 m. The door leaves are of plywood with 2 mm aluminium cladding with stove-enamelled colour finish, black, yellow and various shades of red on the outside, black, yellow and green on the inside.

Wohnhaus des Architekten. Auf die Sperrholztür, 1,00 × 2,00 m groß, wurde 2 mm starkes Aluminiumblech aufgeschraubt. Das Aluminiumblech ist einbrennlackiert.

Maler Diether F. Domes, Langenargen
Architekt Eugen Benninger, Friedrichshafen

The Architect's house. 2 mm thick aluminium sheet was screwed to the plywood door, 1.00 × 2.00 m. The aluminium sheet has a stove-enamelled finish.

Eingangstür des Vita-Hauses in Stuttgart. Türgröße 1,20 × 2,00 m. Auf den Stahlrahmen sind von beiden Seiten je drei Tafeln aus tief blau emailliertem Stahlblech aufgeschraubt, die an den Kanten umgebördelt wurden. Griffloch 15 × 15 cm. Bodentürschließer.

Maler Kurt Frank, Tübingen
Architekt Wilfried Beck-Erlang, Stuttgart

Entrance door to the Vita House, Stuttgart. Door dimensions 1.20 × 2.00 m. Three panels of steel sheet, enamelled deep blue with lapped edges, are screwed on to each side of the steel framing. Handle recess 15 × 15 cm. Floor closer.

Wohnhaus Kraft, Bleichenbach, Hessen. Die Sperrholztür, 1,00 × 2,00 m, ist mit 2 mm Aluminiumblech bekleidet, im Falz geschraubt. Das Aluminium ist einbrennlackiert.

Entwurf Diether F. Domes, Langenargen
Architekt H. Kraft, Bleichenbach/Hessen

The Architects house, Bleichenbach, Hessen. The plywood door, 1.00 × 2.00 m, has 2 mm aluminium sheet cladding screwed into the rebate. The aluminium is stove-enamelled.

Wohnhaus in Stuttgart. Auf der Haustür, einem abgesperrten Türblatt 0,97 × 1,97 m, ist außen mit Bettbeschlägen eine 18 mm dicke Furnierplatte eingehängt, die mit 2 mm Aluminiumblech bekleidet ist. Bemalung mit Einbrennlack. Innenseite der Tür wie Stockrahmen blau gestrichen. Türgriff außen eingeschraubter Ring aus Edelstahl 8 mm.

Maler Diether F. Domes, Langenargen
Architekt Hermann Jürgen Eckert, Stuttgart

Detached house, Stuttgart. On the front door, a flush door leaf 0.97 × 1.97 m has underlays of 18 mm thick veneered panels, clad with 2 mm aluminium sheet. Colour effects by stove enamelling. Door interior and storey frame painted blue. Door handle is an externally screwed on ring of 8 mm stainless steel.

Kath. Kirche St. Petrus, Bamberg-Walsdorf. Das zweiflügelige Hauptportal ist 2,45 × 2,60 m groß. Auf dem Stahlrahmen sind je 3 Stahlblechtafeln befestigt, die außen ultramarinblau, rot, weiß und grau, innen weiß und schwarz emailliert sind. Befestigung mit Spezialkleber in vorgefertigte Falze.

Entwurf Herbert Bessel, Rasch bei Nürnberg
Architekt Bernhard Heid, Fürth

R. Cath. Church of St. Peter, Bamberg-Walsdorf. Dimensions of the double-leaf main portal are 2.45 × 2.60 m. Three sheet steel panels are attached to each steel frame, enamelled on the outside ultramarine blue, red, white and grey, on the inside white and black. Attachment by special adhesive in the prefabricated rebate.

Rathaus Pforzheim. Tür zum Standesamt. Die Türflügel sind jeweils 1,00 × 2,10 m groß. Sie tragen auf einer Holz-Unterkonstruktion handpolierte Aluminiumgußplatten, in die die Aussparungen für die emaillierten Flächen eingeschnitten sind. Die in Rot und Blau gehaltene Arbeit zeichnet sich durch malerische Farbübergänge (nur wenige die Farbübergänge eingrenzende Stege) aus. Sie ist in ihrer freien Gestaltung auf eine gegenüberliegende Wandgestaltung abgestimmt.

Entwurf Irmgard Leuser, Pforzheim
Architekt Rudolf Prenzel, Stuttgart

Town Hall, Pforzheim. Door to the Registry Office. The door leaves each measure 1.00 × 2.10 m. They have a wood sub-structure supporting hand-polished, cast aluminium plates, recessed to take the enamelled surfaces. The design in red and blue is characterized by subtle colour transitions (only few adhere strictly to the web delineated). The free artistry harmonizes with a mural opposite.

1 vorgespanntes Glas 12 mm
2 Akryl, rot opak
3 Dichtung
4 Messinghalbrohr, verchromt
5 Zuggriff
6 Stoßgriff

1 12 mm security glass
2 Acrylic, opaque red
3 Sealing
4 Brass split pipe, chromium-plated
5 Pull handle
6 Push plate

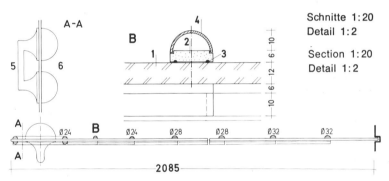

Schnitte 1:20
Detail 1:2

Section 1:20
Detail 1:2

2085

Rathaus Pforzheim. Die inneren und äußeren Türen der Windfänge sind gleich: jeweils zwei Flügel aus 12 mm Sicherheitsglas sind mit Streifen aus rotem Akrylglas und Halbrohren aus verchromtem Messing belegt (Befestigung mit Edelstahlschrauben). Dabei sitzen die waagrechten Streifen außen, die senkrechten innen, so daß sich ein mit der Bewegung wechselndes Linienspiel ergibt. Flügelmaß 1,10 × 2,50 m, Gesamtfläche 4,58 × 2,50 m. Griffe aus Messing, verchromt.

Entwurf Studio Krause, Pforzheim
Architekt Rudolf Prenzel, Stuttgart

Town Hall, Pforzheim. The inner and outer vestibule doors are the same: each comprises two wings of 12 mm safety glass laid with strips of red acrylic glass and split pipes of chromium-plated brass. The horizontal strips are on the outside, the vertical ones on the inside, so that with movement there is an alternating play of lines. Wing dimensions 1.10 × 2.50 m, overall area 4.58 × 2.50 m. Handle of brass, chromium-plated.

Haupteingang einer Schule in München-Perlach. Rahmenkonstruktion aus Leichtmetallprofilen. Füllungen aus einbrennlackiertem Stahlblech. Türgröße etwa 2,20 × 2,60 m.

Entwurf Manfred Mayerle und Andreas Sobeck, München
Architekten H. v. Werz, J. C. Ottow, E. Bachmann, M. Marx, München

Main entrance to a school at Munich-Perlach. Frames designed in light metal section. Panels of stove-enamelled, steel sheet. Door dimensions approx. 2.20 × 2.60 m.

Gesamtschule Stuttgart-Neugereut. Die Eingangstüren sind Leichtmetallkonstruktionen, deren Innen- und Außenflächen gelb einbrennlackiert sind. Gesamtmaß 2,30 × 2,10 m. Vor den Türen stehen Vordächer, deren Schalen aus gelbem, glasfaserverstärktem Kunststoff bestehen.

Architekten B. Perlia, H. W. Schliebitz, J. Schwarz, Stuttgart

Comprehensive school, Stuttgart-Neugereut. The entrance doors of light metal construction, with the interior and exterior surfaces stove-enamelled in yellow. Overall dimensions 2.30 × 2.10 m. Canopies in front of the doors are of yellow, glass-fibre reinforced plastics construction.

Feierhalle des Krematoriums Leinfelden, Zweiflügelige, stumpf einschlagende Tür. Unterkonstruktion aus Stahlrohren, mit dunkelbraun eloxiertem Aluminium verkleidet. Flügelmaß 1,10 × 2,20 m. Die Flügel tragen ein- oder beidseitig farbig lackierte Aluminiumtafeln. Die Außentüren sind in Grün und Blau gehalten, die gleich gestaltete Tür zum Krematoriumsraum in Blau und Rotlila.

Entwurf Karl Pfahler, Fellbach bei Stuttgart
Architekten Max Bächer und Harry G. H. Lie, Stuttgart

Ceremonial hall of Leinfelden Crematorium. Double-wing, flush door. Sub-structure of tubular steel with dark-brown, anodized aluminium cladding. Wing dimensions 1.10 × 2.20 m. The door leaves have panels of painted aluminium on one or both sides. The external doors are simply in blue and green and the door of similar design to the crematorium hall in blue and reddish-lilac.

1	Aluminium 3 mm	Ansicht und Grundriß 1:50
2	Stahlrohr 40/40/3 mm	Detail 1:5
3	Aluminium	
4	Aluminium 4 mm, Kanten abgerundet	
5	Aluminium 6 mm, Kanten abgerundet	
6	Zapfenbänder	

1	3 mm aluminium	Elevation and ground plan 1:50
2	Steel tube 40/40/3 mm	Detail 1:5
3	Aluminium	
4	4 mm aluminium, rounded edges	
5	6 mm aluminium, rounded edges	
6	Mortise hinges	

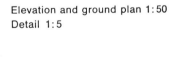

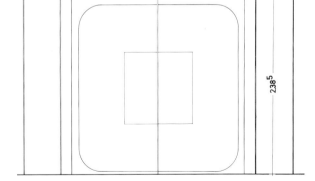

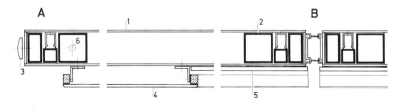

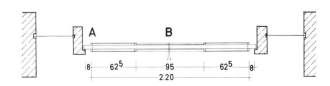

Wohnzentrum Kleinhadern, München. Die Türen zu den verschiedenen Treppenhäusern sind Metallkonstruktionen, 1,06 × 2,10 m groß, und mit farbig emailliertem Stahlblech bekleidet. Die Grundfarben — rot, blau, gelb — wechseln je nach Gebäudeteil. Die Figuren sind nach Kollagen im Maßstab 1:1 im Siebdruck aufgebracht und eingebrannt. Siehe auch Seite 57 oben.
Entwurf Manfred Mayerle und Andreas Sobeck, München
Architekt Peter Lanz, München

Neighbourhood unit, Kleinhadern, Munich. The doors to the different staircases are of metal construction, 1.06 × 2.10 m in size, with steel sheet enamelled in colours. The ground colours — red, blue, yellow — vary according to the different blocks. The figures are applied as screen printed collages, scale 1:1, and stove-enamelled. See also page 57, top.

Gesamtschule an der Freudstraße, München. Allen Türen liegt ein gemeinsames formales Konzept zugrunde: die bei den Eingangstüren verglasten Flächen sind bei den Flurtüren undurchsichtig und umgekehrt. Rahmenkonstruktion aus Stahlrohren. Flächen mit 2 mm Aluminiumblech bekleidet. Gelbe Einbrennlackierung. Je nach Gebäudeteil ist das Feld in der Mitte grün, weiß oder rot. Türmaß außen ca. 2,20 × 2,70 m, innen ca. 2,20 × 2,05 m.
Entwurf Manfred Mayerle und Andreas Sobeck, München
Architekt Erhard Fischer, München

Comprehensive school, Munich. A basic formal design is common to all the doors. The glazed areas in the entrance doors are opaque in the corridor doors and vice versa. Tubular steel framing. Cladding of 2 mm aluminium sheet on non-glazed surfaces. Yellow stove-enamelling. According to the particular area of the building the middle bay is green, white or red. Door dimensions: external approx. 2.20 × 2.70 m, internal approx. 2.20 × 2.05 m.

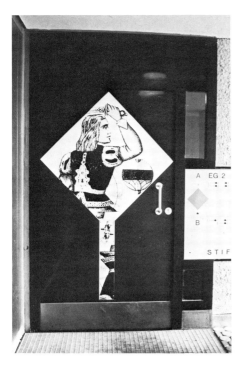  

Universitätsbibliothek Erlangen. Zwei zweiflügelige Metalltüren führen zum Windfang. Türmaß etwa 2,50 × 2,65 m. Metallkonstruktion mit Einbrennlackierung in Weiß und Dunkelblau. Die Türen sind als durchschreitbares Zeichen zwischen außen und innen aufgefaßt.

Entwurf Manfred Mayerle und Andreas Sobeck, München
Architekt Universitätsbauamt Erlangen

University library, Erlangen. Two double-leaf metal doors lead to the vestibule. Door dimensions approx. 2.50 × 2.65 m. Metal construction with stove-enamelling in white and dark blue. The doors are conceived as a symbolic threshold between the inner and outer world.

Medizinische Institute der Universität Heidelberg. Zweiflügelige Eingangstür, Durchgangsflügel jeweils rechts. Zapfenbänder mit Bodentürschließer. Flächige Stahlblechkonstruktion, kräftig blau lackiert. Stoßgriffe aus rostfreiem Stahlrohr ⌀ 30 mm.
Architekt Universitätsbauamt Heidelberg

Medical Institute, Heidelberg University. Double-wing entrance door, swing door leaf on right. Mortise hinges with floor closers. Flush steel sheet construction, painted deep blue. Push bars of stainless steel, 30 mm dia.

Hauseingangstür in München. Das Türfeld ist mit Amco-Blechen (Leichtmetall) bekleidet. Die Hausnummer ist in fast 3 m hohen Ziffern grün aufemailliert. Eine Klingel ist in den Gehflügel eingebaut und durch schwarze konzentrische Kreise und einen schwarzen Pfeil markiert. Die Tür ist in der gesamten Breite zu öffnen.
Entwurf Manfred Mayerle und Andreas Sobeck, München
Architekt H. Peter Buddeberg, München

Entrance to a block of flats, Munich. The bays have light metal sheet cladding. The house number appears in green enamelled figures almost 3 m high. A bell is incorporated in the swing leaf and marked by black, concentric circles and a black arrow. The door is openable to its full width.

Verwaltungsgebäude in Filderstadt-Bonlanden. Das Sperrholztürblatt, 1,10 × 2,00 m groß, ist mit kobaltblau emailliertem Stahlblech (RAL 5013) belegt. Verschraubung seitlich. Anschlag mit Zapfenbändern, Bodentürschließer. Die Tür schlägt stumpf in einen Stahlrahmen, der nach außen kaum in Erscheinung tritt. Windfangwände Ganzglaskonstruktion. Das Edelstahlblech mit Klingel, Sprechanlage und Posteinwurf nimmt die Breite des Türgriffs auf.

Architekt Wilfried Beck-Erlang, Stuttgart

Administration building at Filderstadt-Bonlanden. The plywood door leaf, measuring 1.10 × 2.00 m, is covered in cobalt blue enamelled, steel sheets. Screwed connection at side. Hanging stile with mortise hinges, floor closer. The door closes flush with a steel frame which from the outside is hardly visible. Fully glazed vestibule wall. The stainless steel sheet component with bell, intercom and letter-box conforms to the width of the door handle.

Bürogebäude des Siedlungswerks der Diözese Rottenburg, Stuttgart. Zweiflügelige Tür, Größe 2,58 × 2,07 m. Rahmen aus Stahlrohr 50/50/4 mm, mit 3 mm Stahlblech bekleidet. Die Bleche sind auf der innenliegenden Seite mit Mennige gestrichen, außen spritzverzinkt und mit olivgrünem Akryl-Lack gestrichen. Zwischen den Türgriffen wurde 14 mm 3-Scheiben-Verbundglas eingesetzt.

Architekten Rainer Zinsmeister und Giselher Scheffler, Stuttgart

Office building of the Rottenburg Diocesan Settlement, Stuttgart. Double-leaf door, dimensions 2.58 × 2.07 m. Tubular steel frame 50/50/4 mm, with 3 mm steel sheet cladding. The sheets are painted on the interior with lead oxide red and on the outside spray-galvanized and given an olive-green, acrylic paint coating. 3-piece laminated glass, 14 mm thick, inset between the door handles.

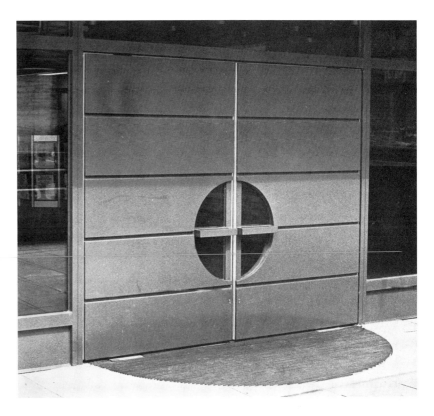

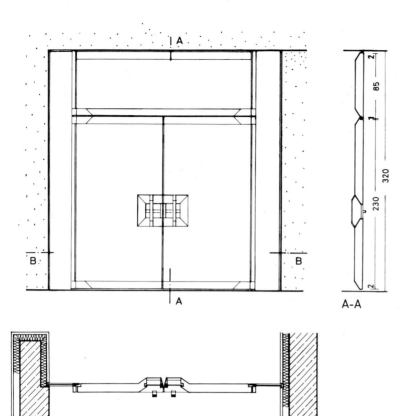

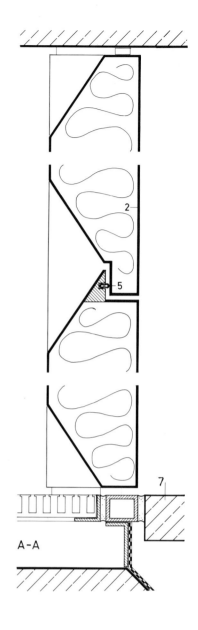

A-A

Ansicht und Grundriß 1:50
Schnitte 1:5

1 U 120
2 2,5 mm Stahlblech
3 Stahlrohr 80/40/4 mm
4 10 mm Dickglas
5 Neoprene-Dichtung
6 Stahl 40/20 mm, Kanten abgerundet
7 Betonpflaster

Elevation and ground plan 1:50
Section 1:5

1 Channel 120
2 2.5 mm steel sheet
3 Tubular steel 80/40/4 mm
4 10 mm thick sheet glass
5 Neoprene sealing
6 40/20 mm steel, rounded edges
7 Concrete paving

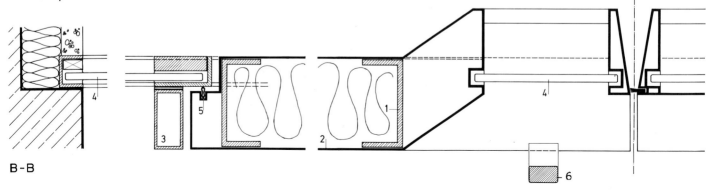

B-B

Kath. Kirche St. Josef, Stuttgart. Zweiflügelige Tür aus Stahlblech auf Profilstahlrahmen. Anschlag mit verkleideten Zapfenbändern, Bodentürschließer. Türblätter und Anschlagrahmen sind blaugrau lackiert.
Architekten Rainer Zinsmeister und Giselher Scheffler, Stuttgart

R. Cath. Church of St. Joseph, Stuttgart. Double-leaf door of steel sheet in profiled steel frame. Mortise hinges with cladding, floor closers. Door leaves and jambs painted blue-grey.

Feierhalle Friedhof Ostfildern in Stuttgart-Sillenbuch. Unterkonstruktion des Türblattes aus Rechteckstahlrohr 60/40/2 mm, beidseitig mit 2 mm Stahlblech bekleidet. Stumpf aufschlagende Tür mit Bodentürschließer und Panikverschluß, in verschiedenen Grüntönen lackiert. Flügelmaß 1,40 × 2,12 m.
Architekten Rainer Zinsmeister und Giselher Scheffler, Stuttgart

Ceremonial Hall, Ostfildern Cemetery at Stuttgart-Sillenbuch. Sub-structure of door leaf in rectangular tubular steel 60/40/2 mm, with 2 mm steel sheet cladding on both sides. Flush door with floor closer and panic bolt, painted in different shades of green. Wing dimensions 1.40 × 2.12 m.

Portal der Berliner Stadtbibliothek. Stahl-Glas-Konstruktion, 6,00 × 4,10 m, in die zwei zweiflügelige Türen integriert sind (Flügelmaß 2 × 5 Felder = 0,90 × 2,20 m). In das Gitterwerk sind 117 geschmiedete Platten ca. 25 × 25 cm eingesetzt, die den Buchstaben A in den verschiedensten Variationen tragen. Die Platten sind teilweise mit Kupfer oder Messing beschmolzen, blattvergoldet oder durch Anlaßfarben getönt.

Portal, Berlin City Library. Steel and glass construction system, 6.00 × 4.10 m, incorporating two double-leaf doors (wing dimensions 2 × 5 bays = 0.90 × 2.20 m). Inset in the grille are 117 wrought steel plates, each bearing a different variation of the letter "A". Parts of the plates also include molten copper or brass, gold leaf or annealing colour decoration.

Entwurf und Ausführung Fritz Kühn †

Landeszentralbank NRW und Hauptverwaltung der Deutschen Bundesbank, Düsseldorf. Die Tür zum Sitzungssaal ist zweiflügelig, Türblattgröße 1,20 × 3,22 m, 12 cm dick. Sichtflächen sind zwei 8 mm starke Stahlbleche, die durch Ätzung strukturiert und brüniert wurden. Punktweise Auflagen aus Blattsilber und Blattgold. Unterkonstruktion aus kräftigen Stahlprofilen, an denen die Deckbleche unsichtbar (durch hinten angeschweißte Stahlprofile, die im Stoß verschraubt sind) befestigt sind. Anschlagdichtung Moosgummi und Bürsten. Dämmung durch eingelegte bzw. innen aufgeklebte Isoliermatten. Wegen des großen Türgewichtes wurden zum Anschlag Bänder aus dem Tresorbau verwendet.

Entwurf und Ausführung Fritz Kühn †
Architekten Dr.-Ing. F. W. Kraemer, G. Pfennig, E. Sieverts, Braunschweig

Central Regional Bank of North Rhineland-Westphalia, Dusseldorf. The double-wing door to the Conference Hall has dimensions of 1.20 × 3.22 m × 12 cm thick. Faced with two 8 mm thick, steel sheets, textured by etching and burnished. Stippling of gold and silver leaf. Sub-structure of robust steel sections with concealed attachment to facing (steel sections welded to back of sheet and screwed at end). Jamb sealing with foam rubber and nylon brush weatherstrip. Insulation by loose inserts or attached insulating quilt. Strongroom hinges used because of great weight of door.

Stadtbibliothek Berlin, Detail
Berlin City Library, detail

Kröpeliner Tor, Rostock. In diesem ehemaligen Stadttor im Westen der Altstadt ist heute das Museum für Stadtgeschichte untergebracht. Die zweiflügelige Eingangstür steht in einer von schlanken Stahlprofilen gehaltenen Ganzglasfläche. Die Türblätter, zusammen 1,80 × 2,10 m groß, sind mit Stahlplatten bekleidet, die mit Kupfer und Messing beschmolzen sind. Zwischenfläche aus 10 mm Sicherheitsglas.

Entwurf und Ausführung Achim Kühn, Berlin-Grünau

Kroepelin Gate, Rostock. The municipal History Museum is today housed in the former City Gate in the west of the Old Town. The double-wing entrance door stands in a fully glazed surround supported by slender steel sections. The door leaves, together 1.80 × 2.10 m in area, are faced with steel plates with molten copper and brass surface finish. 10 mm safety glass strips between.

Eingangstür zum Studentenklub im ehemaligen mittelalterlichen Pulverturm von Weimar. In dem zweischaligen Türblatt ist eine 20 mm dicke Scheibe aus Sicherheitsglas eingearbeitet. Turmaß 0,90 × 2,03 m. Außen- und Innenfläche bestehen aus 4 mm Stahlblech, chemisch behandelt, stahlfarben lasiert. Anschlag mit Zapfenband bzw. Bodentürschließer, Zarge als Sonderprofil.

Entwurf und Ausführung Achim Kühn, Berlin-Grünau

Entrance door to the Students' Union in the former mediaeval Powder Tower in Weimar. A 20 mm thick strip pane of safety glass is incorporated in the double-skin door leaf. Door dimensions. 0.90 × 2.03 m. Interior and exterior surfaces of 4 mm steel sheet, chemically treated, with steel coloured glaze. Mortise hinge and floor closer. Specially profiled trim.

63

Eingangstür einer Gaststätte in München. Gesamtmaß 2,40 × 2,60 m. Die beiden Flügel haben einen umlaufenden Rahmen aus geschmiedetem Vierkantstahl. Die Füllungen bestehen aus abgekanteten und überschmiedeten Blechstreifen von 5 mm Stärke. Die beiden Drückerplatten sind durch eingemeißelte Ornamente verziert.

Entwurf und Ausführung Manfred und German Bergmeister, Ebersberg

Entrance door to a restaurant in Munich. Overall dimensions 2.40 × 2.60 m. The two wings have a surrounding frame of wrought, square bar steel. The panels consist of chamfered, lap-seamed strips, 5 mm thick. The two push pads are ornamented with an incised design.

Eingangsportal am Kloster Waldkirch bei Waldshut.
Das zweiflügelige Portal ist ca. 2,20 × 2,40 m groß und
aus Bronze gearbeitet. Der kräftige Rahmen trägt ein
Gitter, das aus Vierkantbronzestäben 40/20 mm geschmiedet ist. Überkreuzungen breit gezogen und verschweißt.

Entwurf und Ausführung Manfred und German Bergmeister, Ebersberg

Entrance portal to the Waldkirch convent at Waldshut. The double-leaf portal is approx. 2.20 × 2.40 m
in size, of wrought bronze. The powerful frame
supports a grille of forged, square bronze bars,
40/20 mm. The intersections are flattened and spot-
welded.

Wohnhauseingang in Mainz, Umbau. Rahmenkonstruktion aus Stahlhohlprofilen, mattschwarz gestrichen. Verglasung mit Ornamentglas-Thermopane.
Tür 1,15 × 2,18 m, feststehende Seitenteile je 0,90 m
breit. Vor jedem der drei Felder steht ein kunstge-
schmiedetes Gitter, Ausgangsmaterial Vierkantstahl
20/70 mm. Die Gitter sind mit Zinkchromat grundiert
und matt schwarz gespritzt.

Entwurf und Ausführung Hermann Gradinger, Mainz

Door to a detached house, Mainz, conversion. Hollow
steel sectional frame, painted matt black. "Thermopane" decorative, insulating glazing. Door 1.15 ×
2.18 m, fixed side elements 0.90 m wide respectively.
An artistic, wrought steel grille of square bar steel,
20/70 mm, stands in front of each of the 3 bays.
The grilles have a zinc chromate priming with
sprayed, matt black top coat.

Eingangsportal der kath. Kirche St. Helena, München. Gesamtmaß ca. 3,30 × 3,00 m. Die Flügel sind mit Bronzeblech beschlagen und durch eingelegte Streifen aus farbigem Gußglas (Gangkofner, Zwiesel) verziert.

Entwurf und Ausführung Manfred und German Bergmeister, Ebersberg

Entrance portal of the R. Cath. Church of St. Helena, Munich. Overall dimensions approx. 3.30 × 3.00 m. The wings have bronze sheet facings decorated with inlaid strips of coloured, cast glass (Gangkofner, Zwiesel).

Zweiflügeliges Türgitter am Eingang eines Einfamilienhauses. Die beiden Gitterteile messen zusammen 2,80 × 2,20 m und sind aus Vierkantstahl 20/20 mm gearbeitet. Die Stäbe sind an den Überkreuzungen breitgeschmiedet und von hinten miteinander verschweißt. Das Gitter ist mit 5 cm Abstand am Rahmen der dahinter stehenden verglasten Tür befestigt.

Entwurf und Ausführung Hermann Gradinger, Mainz

Double-leaf door grille at the entrance to a private house. The two grille sections, dimensions together 2.80 × 2.20 m, are of square bar steel. The bars are flattened at the intersections and spot-welded from the back. The grille is tied to the frame of the glazed door standing 5 cm behind it.

Ausbildungszentrum der Schweizerischen Bankgesellschaft, Ermatingen/Schweiz. Der Haupteingang ist eine zweiflügelige Tür, Gesamtmaß 2,50 × 2,12 m. Unterkonstruktion des Rahmens Rechteckstahlrohr 120/50/5 mm. Bekleidung des Rahmens und aufgesetzte Profile aus geschmiedetem Bronzeblech. Dabei wurden die einzelnen Blechflächen mit Kartonschablonen am Modell 1:1 abgenommen und entsprechend geschmiedet und getrieben, Nähte schutzgas-verschweißt. Verglasung mit Dickglasscheibe in Messing-U-Profil. Anschlag mit Zapfenbändern bzw. Bodentürschließer.
Entwurf Ernst Burgdorfer, Zürich
Architekten Rudolf und Esther Guyer, Zürich

Training Centre of the Swiss Banking Company, Ermatingen, Switzerland. The main entrance consists of a 2-leaf door with overall dimensions of 2.50 × 2.12 m. The frame base is of rectangular steel tube 120/50/5 mm. Cladding of frame and exposed sections of wrought bronze sheet. For this individual metal sheets were marked out with cardboard templates, scale 1:1, and correspondingly wrought and chased. The seams were inert-gas welded. Thick window glazing in rolled brass channels. Hung on mortise hinges and with floor closers.

Juweliergeschäft in Wien. Rahmenkonstruktion aus Rechteckstahlrohren, mit Stahlblech verstärkt und außen mit verschiedenfarbigen Messingblechen bekleidet, innen mit Leder bespannt. Füllung aus 26 mm Panzerglas. Griffe Chromnickelstahl. Das Türblatt mißt 0,75 × 2,09 m. Die Rohre im Durchbruch über der Tür sind Luftansaugöffnungen der Klimaanlage.

Architekt Hans Hollein, Wien ▷

Jeweller's shop, Vienna. Frame designed in rectangular steel tube reinforced with steel sheet and clad externally with brass sheets in various colours, on the interior leather-covered. Panels of 26 mm bullet-proof glass. Handles of chrome-nickel steel. Door leaf dimensions 0.75 × 2.09 m. The pipes in the opening over the door are air discharge outlets for the air conditioning plant.

Eingangstür zu einem Wohnhaus. Gesamtmaß 0,98 × 2,10 m. Rahmen und Vergitterung aus 15 bis 25 mm dicken Kupferplatten geschweißt und dann patiniert. Dahinter liegt eine 8 mm dicke Rohglasscheibe.

Entwurf und Ausführung Werkkunst Peters, Stolberg

Entrance door to a detached house. Overall dimensions 0.98 × 2.10 m. Frame and lattice-work of 15 to 25 mm thick copper sheets welded and then anodized. The glazing behind is of 8 mm thick sheet glass.

Ladeneingang der Firma Pelz-Maier in Stuttgart. In das Eingangsfeld, 2,00 × 3,20 m, ist ein freistehender Blockrahmen aus Stahlprofilen gestellt, der mit 0,6 mm Kupferblech bekleidet wurde. Ganzglastür und Glasfeld aus 12 mm Parsol Bronze (Sekurit), Innenflächen matt geätzt. Flügelmaß 1,10 × 2,50 m. Türanschlag oben Zapfenbänder, unten Bodentürschließer Stop. Umlaufendes Gummiprofil im Rahmen. Kupferblech matt gebürstet und durch farblose Lackierung vor Korrosion geschützt.

Architekt Bernhard Kolditz, Reutlingen

Furrier's shop. Stuttgart. The free-standing, steel sectional, block frame in the entrance panel, 2.00 × 3.20 m, has 0.6 mm copper sheet cladding. All-glass door and glazed bay of 12 mm. Parsol Bronze (Securit), inner surfaces matt etched. Wing dimensions 1.10 × 2.50 m. Above mortise hinges, below floor closer door stay. Surrounding rubber weatherstrip in frame. Copper sheet satinized and corrosion protected with transparent varnish.

1 Stahlblech 2 mm
2 Furnierplatte 6 mm
3 Korkauflage 2 mm
4 Lederbespannung 1 mm
5 Mineralwolle 40 mm
6 Messingblech 1,5 mm
7 Stahlblech 3 mm, schwer bohrbar
8 Kittbett
9 Panzerglas mit Alarmdrahteinlage 26 mm
10 Messingblech 2 mm
11 Stahlrohr 25/25/2 mm
12 Naturstein, poliert

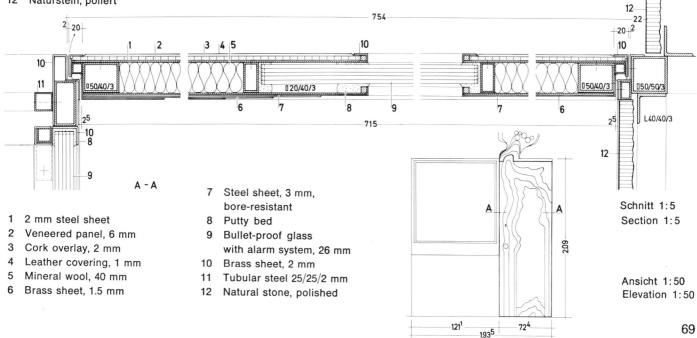

A - A

1	2 mm steel sheet	7	Steel sheet, 3 mm, bore-resistant
2	Veneered panel, 6 mm	8	Putty bed
3	Cork overlay, 2 mm	9	Bullet-proof glass with alarm system, 26 mm
4	Leather covering, 1 mm	10	Brass sheet, 2 mm
5	Mineral wool, 40 mm	11	Tubular steel 25/25/2 mm
6	Brass sheet, 1.5 mm	12	Natural stone, polished

Schnitt 1:5
Section 1:5

Ansicht 1:50
Elevation 1:50

69

Kath. Kirche St. Johannes in Hornberg/Schwarzwald. Die Türflügel sind 1,70 × 2,40 m groß und 80 mm dick. Unterkonstruktion Edelstahlrohre 80/40/2 mm. Von beiden Seiten mit 1,5 mm Edelstahlblech belegt. In beide Bleche sind in einem Raster von 240 × 240 mm Durchbrüche von 150 mm ⌀ herausgestanzt und durch eingeschweißte „Büchsen" aus Edelstahl verbunden. Die Hohlräume wurden ausgeschäumt. In die Büchsen sind außen und innen formgeschmolzene Farbgläser eingesetzt. Die Stahlbleche sind mehrfach überschliffen. Die Drehachse ist von der Außenkante 40 cm nach innen gelegt, Anschlag mit überschweren Zapfenbändern; Bodentürschließer.

Entwurf und Ausführung Glas + Form F. Lechner, Neubeuern
Architekt Rainer Disse, Karlsruhe

R. Cath. Church of St. John, Hornberg, Black Forest. The door leaves are 1.70 × 2.40 m in area and 80 mm thick. Core of stainless steel tubes 80/40/2 mm. Faced on both sides with stainless steel sheet. Both sheets have perforations of 150 mm dia. punched in a grid measuring 240 × 240 mm, with welded-on eyelet liners of stainless steel. The cavities are foam-filled. The liners are set inside and out with moulded, coloured glass. The steel sheets were surface polished several times. The pivot hinge is set toward the inside, 40 cm from the outside edge. Hung on heavy-duty mortise hinges; floor closers.

Kath. Kirche in Oftersheim. Zweiflügelige Tür, 2,03 × 2,41 m, Stahl-konstruktion mit brüniertem Messing bekleidet. In die Felder sind ringförmige Elemente aus Kupferblech eingesetzt, deren Innen-flächen wie die Zwischenfelder aus farbigem Akrylglas bestehen.
Entwurf Studio Krause, Pforzheim

R. Cath. Church at Oftersheim. Double-leaf door, 2.03 × 2.41 m. Steel construction faced with burnished brass. Annular, copper sheet units are set in the door bays. The inner surfaces of these and the intermediary ground are of coloured acrylic.

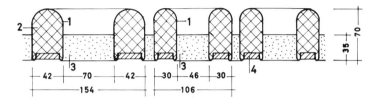

Detail 1:5

1 Kupferblech 1 mm
2 Polyurethanschaum
3 Akryl, farbig, transparent
4 Akryl, farbig, opak

Detail 1:5

1 1 mm copper sheet
2 Polyurethane foam
3 Acrylic, coloured, transparent
4 Acrylic, coloured, opaque

Pelzgeschäft in Frankfurt/M. Die Schaufensterfront ist im Eingangs-bereich halbkreisförmig eingezogen und besteht wie die Türscheibe aus 12 mm Akrylglas. Türrahmen, Griffblende und Zarge aus Edel-stahl, gebürstet. Türmaß 1,00 × 2,00 m.
Architekt Bernhard Kilb, Dreieichenhain

Furrier's shop, Frankfurt/Main. The display window curves in-wards, in half-moon shape, towards the door. Door panes and frontage are of 12 mm acrylic glass. Door frame, handle cross-bar and trim are of satinized, stainless steel. Door dimensions 1.00 × 2.00 m.

Eingang eines Mehrfamilienhauses, Düsseldorf. Rahmen der verglasten Eingangstür, Seitenflächen und Garagentore mit Edelstahlblech bekleidet.
Architekt E. Weil, Düsseldorf

Entrance to a multi-family residential block, Dusseldorf. Frame of glazed entrance door, side panels and garage doors with stainless steel cladding.

Sakristeitür einer Kirche in Krefeld. Rahmen aus Vierkantstahlrohr, mit Edelstahl verkleidet. Unteres Türfeld Drahtglas, oberes Rohglas. Griffblende und Griffstange Edelstahl.
Architekt Heinz Döhmen, Mönchengladbach

Sacristy door of a church in Krefeld. Square bar steel frame, with stainless steel cladding. Lower bay, wired glass — upper bay, sheet glass. Handle bar and edge trim of stainless steel.

Kunstgalerie in Zürich. In die alte Türöffnung wurde eine dreiteilige Konstruktion aus Glas und Stahlblech gestellt, deren mittlerer Teil beweglich ist (Öffnung ca. 2,10 × 2,15 m, Flügelmaß ca. 0,82 × 2,15 m). 8 mm Sicherheitsglas, Zylinderschloß unten rechts.

Architekt René Haubensak, Zürich

Art gallery, Zurich. A 3-component system of glass and steel sheet, with movable middle section, has been installed in the old doorway. (Opening approx. 2.10 × 2.15 m, wing dimensions approx. 0.82 × 2.15 m). 8 mm safety glass, cylindrical lock, bottom right.

Anton Bruckner-Gymnasium, Straubing. Zweiflügelige Pendeltüren aus Leichtmetall. Flügelmaß 1,15 × 2,30 m. Verglasung aus Kristallspiegeldrahtglas. Metallteile dunkelgrün lackiert, durchgehende Stangengriffe aus 48 mm Edelstahlrohr.

Entwurf Manfred Mayerle und Andreas Sobeck, München
Architekten Hans Gollwitzer, Armin Tinnes und Partner, Deggendorf

Anton Bruckner Secondary School, Straubing. Double-leaf swing doors of light metal. Wing dimensions 1.15 × 2.30 m. Polished plate, wired glazing. Metal components painted dark green, continuous cross-bar handle of 48 mm stainless steel tube.

Section N, Shop for Environmental Design, Vienna. The entrance is set back in a passageway of an officially preserved historic house. The door leaves, standing at right-angles to each other, are 0.85 × 2.57 m in size. The entire entrance wall is of rectangular steel tube framing; 8 mm polished plate glass panes, 25 × 25 cm; glazing strips, 8 × 8 mm, of polished brass bar. The complete jamb and closing stile unit A between the door wings is removable to allow transport of wide objects. A cubic, metal-glass box structure rising above the door is used for mounting the spot-lighting of the entrance.

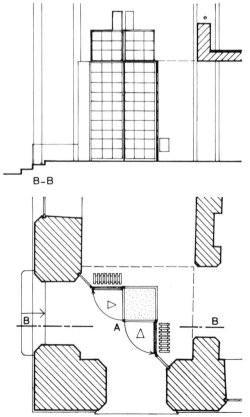

B-B

Section N, Laden für Umweltgestaltung, Wien. Der Eingang liegt etwas zurückgesetzt in der Passage eines unter Denkmalschutz stehenden Hauses. Die rechtwinklig zueinander gestellten Türblätter sind 0,85 × 2,57 m groß. Tragende Konstruktion der gesamten Eingangswand aus Rechteckstahlrohren; 8 mm Spiegelglasscheiben 25 × 25 cm; Glashalteleisten polierter Messingstab 8 × 8 mm. Das gemeinsame Anschlagprofil A zwischen beiden Türflügeln läßt sich herausnehmen, um breitere Gegenstände transportieren zu können. An jeder Tür ist ein würfelförmiger Metall-Glaskasten hochgeführt, auf dem der Scheinwerfer für die Eingangsbeleuchtung montiert ist.

Architekt Hans Hollein, Wien

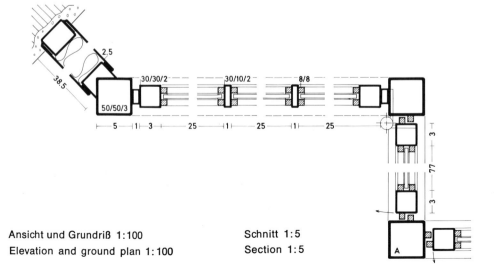

Ansicht und Grundriß 1:100
Elevation and ground plan 1:100

Schnitt 1:5
Section 1:5

Gymnasium in Wertingen. Die Türen der Aula sind mit den anschließenden Wandfeldern, dem Fußboden und der Decke zu einer gestalterischen Einheit entwickelt. Türen Stahlhohlprofile, silberweiß gestrichen.

Entwurf Manfred Mayerle und Andreas Sobeck, München
Architekten Dr.-Ing. Wilhelm Wichtendahl und Partner, Augsburg

Secondary School in Wertingen. The doors of the assembly hall and the adjacent screen walls, floor and ceiling have been combined in a unified design. Steel sectional doors painted silver white.

Kirchliches Zentrum, Jona/Schweiz. Zweiflügelige Eingangstür zum Kirchenraum. Die beiden Flügel sind 1,40 × 2,20 m groß, Konstruktion aus Profilstahlrohr, einfach verglast. Drehpunkt ist die exzentrisch vor dem Türblatt stehende Stange. Stahlteile sandgestrahlt, grundiert und mit dunkelrotem Kunstharzlack gestrichen. Griffstangen verchromt.

Entwurf Benedikt Huber, Zürich
Architekten Huber + Trachsel, Zürich

Church Hall, Jona/Switzerland. Double-leaf entrance door to the area of worship. The two wings, 1.40 × 2.20 m in size are of tubular steel sections, simply glazed. The pivot is the eccentric vertical bar standing in front of the door. Steel components sand blasted, given a primer and coated with a dark red, synthetic resin paint. Door handles chromium-plated.

Gesundheitsamt Dachau. Die Eingangstüren sind wie bei dem Polizeidienstgebäude konstruiert, folgen aber einem anderen formalen Schema, das durch die als Y geführten Griffstangen noch unterstützt wird. Auch die einflügeligen Türen sind nach diesem Schema konzipiert. Die Pflasterung vor dem Eingang nimmt das Motiv des auf die Spitze gestellten Quadrats auf.

Entwurf Manfred Mayerle und Andreas Sobeck, München
Architekt Landbauamt München

Health Office, Dachau. The entrance doors are of similar design to those of the police headquarters, with different formal motifs however, emphasized by the "Y" extension of the handles. The single-leaf hall door also repeats this design with a half-Y. The motif of the square set on the points is repeated in the courtyard paving.

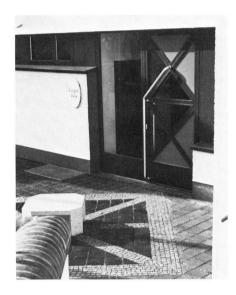

Polizeidienstgebäude Dachau. Zweiflügelige Eingangstür, Flügelmaß 1,07 × 2,04 m. Rahmenkonstruktion aus Aluminiumrohren. Metallteile in Bronzeton einbrennlackiert. Weiß lakkierte Flächen Sandwichplatten (Aludeckbleche, Hartschaumkern). Spiegelglasscheiben 8—10 mm.

Entwurf Manfred Mayerle und Andreas Sobeck, München
Architekt Landbauamt München

Police Headquarters, Dachau. Double-wing entrance door, wing dimensions 1.07 × 2.04 m. Aluminium tubular framing. Metal components stove-enamelled in bronze shades. White-painted sandwich panels (aluminium with rigid foamed polystyrene core). Polished plate glass panes, 8—10 mm.

Krankenhaus Deggendorf. Die Türen übernehmen als Zeichen zugleich eine Hinweisfunktion: Das auf der Spitze stehende Quadrat bezeichnet allgemeine Verkehrswege, ein senkrechtes Quadrat die Stationen und ein Dreieck den Bereich der Ambulanz. — Haupteingang zweiflügelige, automatische Schiebetür, schwarzbraun eloxiertes Leichtmetall, Zeichen auf den Glasflügeln und Füllungen über der Tür leuchtend gelb.

Entwurf Manfred Mayerle und Andreas Sobeck, München
Architekten Köhler-Kässens-Wörner, Frankfurt/M.

Hospital, Deggendorf. The doors have an indicative function, the square on top gives the general circulation direction, a vertical square shows the nursing stations and a triangle stands for an ambulance area. The main doorway has double-wing, automatic sliding doors, in dark-brown anodized light metal. The signs on the glazed wings and overhead panels are in bright yellow.

Ev. Gemeindehaus in Bad Salzuflen-Lockhausen. Die Schiebewand vor der Bühne des Gemeindesaals besteht aus acht Stahlblechelementen von 92 mm Dicke mit schalldämmender Füllung und umlaufenden Dichtungsprofilen (Schalldämmwert der Wand 42 dB). Die Platten wurden nach Angaben der Architekten in drei Rot- und je zwei Gelb-, Grün- und Blautönen lackiert. Gesamtmaß 9,19 × 2,40 m.

Architekten Günter Schmidt und Friedrich Schmersahl, Bad Salzuflen-Lockhausen

Prot. Community Centre in Bad Salzuflen-Lockhausen. The sliding wall in front of the stage of the assembly hall consists of 8 sheet steel units, 92 mm thick with acoustic panels and continuous rubber sealant strip (sound reduction value of wall 42 dB). The panels were painted according to the architects' instructions in 3 shades of red and 2 shades each of yellow, green and blue. Overall dimensions 9.19 × 2.40 m.

Wohnzentrum Kleinhadern, München. Ladeneingangstür in Metallkonstruktion. Leichtmetalldeckprofile dunkel eloxiert, Füllungen in der Tür und oben in der verglasten Front gelb emailliertes Stahlblech. Vergleiche auch Seite 56.

Entwurf Manfred Mayerle und Andreas Sobeck, München

Architekt Peter Lanz, München

Neighbourhood unit, Kleinhadern, Munich. Shop door of metal design, light metal cladding profiles anodized in a dark colour; yellow enamelled, steel sheet panels in and above door of glazed frontage. (Cf. also p. 56).

Städtische Sparkasse Würzburg. Windfang als Ganzglaskonstruktion (Einscheiben-Sicherheitsglas 8—10 mm). In beiden Türfeldern steht zwischen den zwei Flügeltüren ein feststehendes Glasfeld. Aufgeklebte Blechstreifen und Türgriffe polierter Edelstahl. Flügelmaß 1,05 × 2,00 m.

Entwurf Manfred Mayerle und Andreas Sobeck, München

Architekten H. v. Werz, J. Ch. Ottow, M. Marx und E. Bachmann, München

Municipal Savings Bank, Wurzburg. Fully-glazed vestibule doors. Toughened, safety glass, 8—10 mm. A fixed, glazed bay stands between the door wings. Glued-on diagonal strips and door push-pull bar of polished, stainless steel. Wing dimensions, 1.05 × 2.00 m.

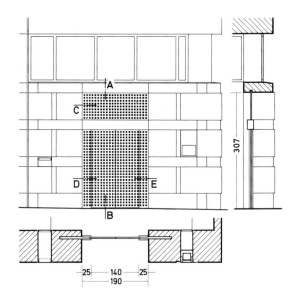

Ansicht 1:100, Schnitte 1:5
Elevation 1:100, Sections 1:5

Haupteingang zur Schalterhalle, Bankhaus Sella & Co. in Biella/Italien. Zweiflügelige Schiebetür, innen Sicherheitsglas, außen mit gestanztem Leichtmetallblech bekleidet. Die Tür wird über Kontaktmatten automatisch gesteuert. Die inneren Seitenflügel können zur Inspektion und Wartung der Türmechanik ausgedreht werden.

Architekten Suter + Suter, Basel

Main entrance to banking hall of the Sella & Co. Bank, Biella, Italy. Double-leaf sliding door, with inner face of safety glass, exterior of perforated, light-alloy sheet cladding. The door is automatically controlled by sensor mats. The interior side wing can be pivoted for inspection and maintenance.

1	Schiebeflügel	10	Leichtmetallprofil
2	Drehflügel, Wartungsflügel	11	Compriband
3	Bankbriefkasten	12	Weißer Carrara-Marmor
4	Nachttresor	13	Pirelli-Gummi
5	Sicherheitsglas		
6	gestanztes Leichtmetallblech, eloxiert		
7	Laufwerk		
8	Türantrieb		
9	Leichtmetallblech, eloxiert		

1	Sliding wing
2	Pivoting wing, maintenance wing
3	Bank mail-box
4	Night safe
5	Safety glass
6	Stamped, light alloy sheet, anodized
7	Sliding door mechanism
8	Door drive system
9	Light metal sheet, anodized
10	Light metal section
11	"Compriband" compressive sealing
12	White Carrara marble
13	Pirelli rubber

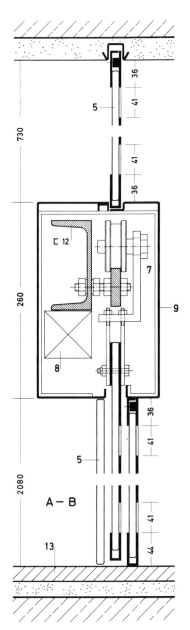

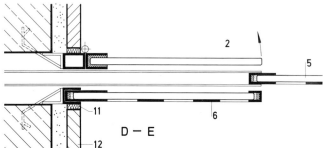

Ersparniskasse Solothurn. Die zweiflügelige Eingangstür hat ein Flügelmaß von 1,30 × 2,60 m. Tragende Konstruktion aus Rechteckstahlrohr. Isolierverglasung. Innen- und Außenseite der Tür sind mit zwei Lagen aus 3 mm Aluminiumblech bekleidet, deren Durchbrüche etwas gegeneinander versetzt sind. Alle Leichtmetallteile farblos eloxiert. Befestigung mit Schrauben aus rostfreiem Stahl. Die Flügel öffnen sich automatisch.

Entwurf F. Maurer, Zürich
Architekt H. Sperisen, Solothurn/Schweiz

Savings Bank, Solothurn. The double-leaf entrance door has a wing dimension of 1.30 × 2.60 m. Load-bearing construction of rectangular tubular steel. Insulating glazing. Inner and outer door surfaces are faced with a double, 3 mm aluminium sheet layer, the slits staggered respectively. All light metal components with colourless anodized finish. Fastening with stainless steel screws. Automatic opening.

Eingangstür für die Niederlage der Firma Omega in Bad Soden. Auf eine Unterkonstruktion aus Rechteckstahlrohr 60/40/2 mm und 40/20/2 mm ist von beiden Seiten eine Verkleidung aus geätztem Leichtmetall gesetzt und im Rahmenfalz verschraubt. Wo die beiden Flügel aneinanderstoßen, ist das schlanke Stahlprofil des Rahmens dunkel gestrichen, so daß die Verglasung über die beiden Flügel durchzulaufen scheint. Türgriffe aus Aluminium geschmiedet. Die Fläche ist 2,90 m hoch, Tür und Glaswand zusammen 3,50 m breit. Verglasung mit 8 mm braun getöntem Sicherheitsglas.

Entwurf Planungsgruppe Jacobs-Kuhnen
Ausführung Hermann Gradinger, Mainz

Entrance door for the Omega Company subsidiary, Bad Soden. Etched, light metal cladding is attached to both sides of the sub-structure of rectangular steel tube 60/40/2 and 40/20/2 mm, and screwed into the frame rebate. At the meeting of the two wings, the slender, steel frame profile is painted in a sombre colour so that the glazing appears to be continuous over the two wings. Door handle of wrought aluminium. The entrance wall is 2.90 m high, door and glazed wall together 3.50 m wide. Glazing of 8 mm brown-tinted safety-glass.

Boutique Christa Metek, Wien. Die Ladenfront ist auf ihrer ganzen Fläche, 4,78 × 4,17 m, mit 2 mm Aluminiumblech bekleidet. Unterkonstruktion Profilstahlrohre. An der Tür, 0,65 × 2,06 m, ist das Aluminiumblech um den Rahmen gekantet und an den Stirnseiten verschraubt. Am Sichtfenster ⌀ 16 cm hinter dem Türgriff aus Edelstahl ist die Bekleidung eingebördelt. Türanschlag mit Bändern, Rohrtürschließer; Schloß im Anschlag montiert. Alle Beschläge Edelstahl.

Architekt Hans Hollein, Wien

Christa Metek Boutique, Vienna. The shopfront has 2 mm aluminium cladding over the entire surface, 4.78 × 4.17 m. Sub-structure of tubular steel sections. At the door, 0.65 × 2.06 m, the aluminium sheet is folded over the frame and screwed at the ends. The cladding has a beaded edging at the vision panel, 16 cm in dia., behind the stainless steel doorhandle. Side-hinged, tubular floor closers. Lock mounted in closing stile. All fittings of stainless steel.

Kerzenladen Retti, Wien. Der schmale Laden ist in einem alten Geschäftshaus eingebaut. Seine Front ist mit matt geschliffenem, natur eloxiertem Aluminiumblech bekleidet, Breite ca. 3,70 m, Höhe ca. 4,50 m. Auf beiden Seiten der vertieft in einer Nische liegenden Tür, Flügelmaß 0,72 × 2,08 m sind kleine Schaukästen angeordnet. Die Leichtmetallbekleidung ist jeweils abgekantet und im Falz bzw. Stoß — von außen unsichtbar — geschraubt. Die Seitenwände der Türnische tragen den Namenszug in rot emaillierten Lettern. Über der Tür ist das Klimagerät installiert. Türanschlag mit Türbändern, Falztürschließer in der Zarge.

Architekt Hans Hollein, Wien

Candle shop Retti, Vienna. The narrow shop is built into an old shop premises. The frontage is clad with satinized, natural anodized, aluminium sheet, width approx. 3.70 m. height approx. 4.50 m. On either side of the doorway, wich is set back in a niche, wing dimensions 0.72 × 2.08 m, are small display windows. The light metal cladding is chamfered and invisibly screwed into the rebate or door stop. The name appears in red enamelled lettering on the inside walls of the door niche. The air conditioning is installed over the door. Side-hinged, rebated closer in door casing.

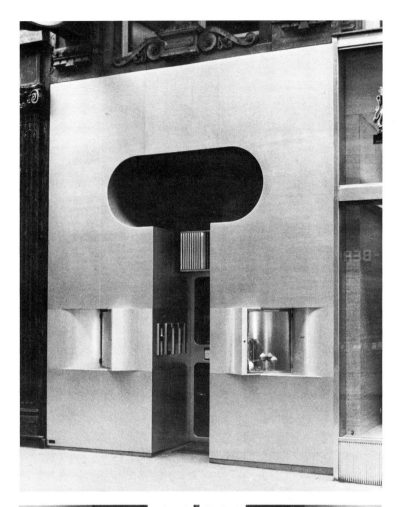

Detail Türanschlag 1:2

1 Aluminiumblech 2 mm
2 Flachstahl 30/10 mm
3 Spiegelglas 6 mm in Neoprenedichtung
4 Stahlrohr 50/30/3 mm
5 Winkelstahl 30/30 mm
6 Gummi

Detail Door rebate 1:2

1 Aluminium sheet, 2 mm
2 Flat bar steel, 30/10 mm
3 Plate glass, 6 mm, in neoprene strip
4 Tubular steel 50/30/3 mm
5 Angle bar steel 30/30 mm
6 Rubber strip

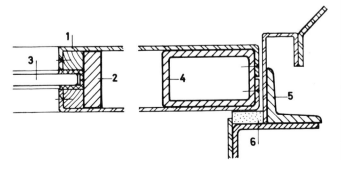

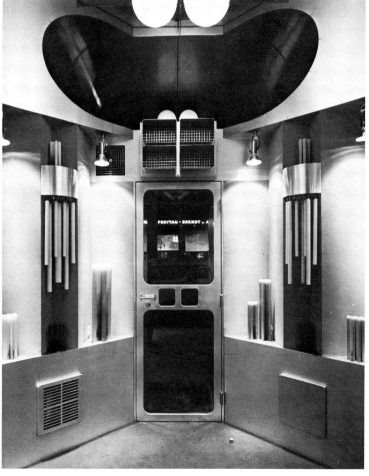

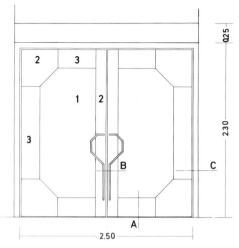

Badisches Staatstheater, Karlsruhe. Zugang zur Eingangs- und Kassenhalle. Rahmenkonstruktion aus Stahlleichtprofilen, Sicherheitsglas und Aluminiumblech-Bekleidung (Glissa). Eckbleche und Blechstreifen auf der Schloßseite natur eloxiert, sonst dunkelgrün. Panikverschluß, Treibriegelschloß mit Schwenkhebel, Bodentürschließer, Türfeststeller.

Architekt Helmut Bätzner, Karlsruhe

Baden State Theatre, Karlsruhe. Access to foyer and booking hall. Light steel sectional framing, safety glass and aluminium sheet cladding. Corner plates and sheet metal strips on the lock side natural anodized, otherwise dark green. Panic bolt, cremorne bolt with swivel handle, floor closer, door stay.

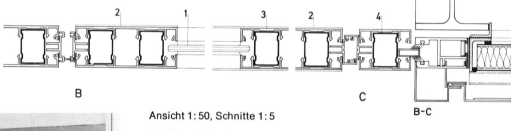

B   C   B-C

Ansicht 1:50, Schnitte 1:5

1 Sicherheitsglas 8—10 mm
2 Leichtmetallblech 3 mm, natur eloxiert
3 Leichtmetallbekleidung, grün gestrichen
4 Stahlleichtprofil
5 Bodentürschließer
6 Natursteinplatten

Elevation 1:50, Sections 1:5

1 Safety glass, 8—10 mm
2 Light metal sheet, 3 mm, natural anodized
3 Light metal cladding, painted green
4 Light steel section
5 Floor closer
6 Natural stone tiles

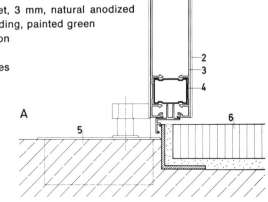

Krematorium Leinfelden. Zweiflügelige Türen, 2,10 × 2,30 m groß, aus 10 mm vorgespanntem Glas. Randbekleidung aus dunkelbraun eloxiertem Leichtmetall, Griffstange aus ⌀ 20 mm Edelstahlrohr, gebürstet.

Architekten Max Bächer und Harry G. H. Lie, Stuttgart

Crematorium, Leinfelden. Double-wing doors, 2.10 × 2.30 m, of 10 mm toughened glass. Edge cladding of dark-brown anodized light metal. Door handle of satinized, stainless steel tube, dia. 20 mm.

Kollegiengebäude der Universität Stuttgart. Der Windfang hat zwei 2flügelige Türpaare. Öffnung jeweils 2,00 × 2,60 m. Rahmenlose Nurglaskonstruktion, Sockelleiste und Griffstange Aluminium natur eloxiert.

Architekten R. Gutbier, C. Siegel, G. Wilhelm, Stuttgart

Lecture Hall, Stuttgart University. The vestibule has a pair of double-wing doors. Opening in each case 2.00 × 2.60 m. All-glass construction without frame. Plinth kicking plate and door handle of natural anodized aluminium.

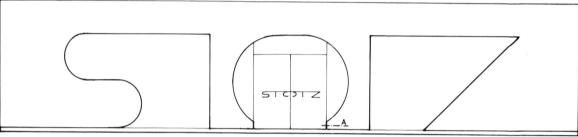

Ansicht 1:100
Elevation 1:100

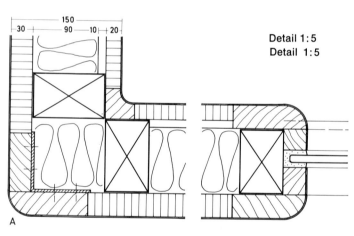

Detail 1:5
Detail 1:5

Schaufensteranlage eines Lampengeschäfts in Stuttgart. Sie zeigt auf etwa 16 m Länge den Firmennamen STOTZ; dabei bildet das O den Eingang, die Formen von ST und TZ sind zu Schaufenstern zusammengefaßt. Der Namenszug tritt auch als Türgriff (Edelstahl) in Erscheinung. Eingang als zweiflügelige Glanzglastüren (15 mm vorgespanntes Glas) mit Bodentürschließer.

Architekten Mögel + Fuhrer, Stuttgart

Display window for a lighting fittings shop in Stuttgart. The firm's name STOTZ extends over approx. 16 metres; the O forms the entrance and the ST and TZ the show windows. The name also appears on the door handle (stainless steel). Entrance with double-leaf, polished glass doors (15 mm toughened glass) with floor closer.

Zweiflügelige Ganzglastüren am umgebauten Stadttheater, Mainz. Oben und unten Türschienen aus brüniertem Messing 100/6 mm. Scheiben 15 mm vorgespanntes Glas, ca. 1,15 × 2,50 m. Türgriffe und Sichtleisten aus rostfreiem Stahl. Der Leuchtkasten über der Tür enthält Leuchtstoffröhren, die auch nach unten auf den Türbereich strahlen.

Ausführung Hermann Gradinger, Mainz
Architekt Dieter Oesterlen, Hannover

Double-leaf, all-glass doors to the rebuilt City Theatre, Mainz. Door rails above and below of burnished brass, 100/6 mm. 15 mm toughened, laminated glass panels, approx. 1.15 × 2.50 m. Door push plates and decorative strips of stainless steel. The box luminaires over the door contain fluorescent tubes which also provide down-lighting.

Marktkirche Hannover, Umbau. Windfangtüren aus 10 – 13 mm Sekurit, gefaßt in 7 mm Messingschienen, dunkel patiniert. Flügelmaß 0,85 × 2,45 m. Griffe: Evangelistensymbole in Bronzeguß.

Architekt Dieter Oesterlen, Hannover

Market Church, Hanover, conversion. Vestibule doors of 10–13 mm safety glass, set in 7 mm brass rails, with dark anodizing. Wing dimensions 0.85 × 2.45 m. Handle: Symbol of the Evangelist in cast bronze.

Zweiflügelige Sekurit-Ganzglastür in der kath. Kirche in Düssel bei Mettmann. Keilschnitt und Flächenschliff. Unteres Drittel dicht gestaltet, nach oben Kreisformen ohne Mattierung in Verbindung mit tief herausgeschliffenen Kreisen, die z. T. poliert sind.

Entwurf Eleonore Lühmann, Köln
Ausführung Werkstätte für Glasgestaltung K. Hirsch
(Walter Hübner), Sprockhövel-Hasslinghausen

Double-wing door fully glazed with safety glass, in the R. Cath. Church, Duessel near Mettmann. Bevelled and intaglio surface. The lower third is thickly patterned with circular motifs without frosting combined with deep-ground circles, partly polished.

Friedhofskapelle in Bitburg-Nord. Ganzglas-Türanlage mit Flächen- und Bandschliff. Die formbestimmenden Bänder sind zusätzlich poliert und dadurch leuchtend.

Entwurf Bruno Spychalski, Hattingen/Ruhr
Ausführung Werkstätte für Glasgestaltung K. Hirsch,
Sprockhövel-Hasslinghausen

Cemetery Chapel, Bitburg-North. Fully glazed door system with surface- and belt-ground finish. The formal glazing strips are specially polished and hence create an effect of light.

Kreissparkasse Neuwied. Eingangstür und Windfang sind Schiebetüren, die über den Tretrost automatisch gesteuert werden. Die Windfangtüren tragen ein handgeschliffenes steingraues Mittelband zur Sichthinderung. Beide Türanlagen sind durch eingeschliffene und polierte Keilschnitte dekoriert.

Entwurf Wilfried Reckewitz, Wuppertal-Barmen
Ausführung Werkstätte für Glasgestaltung K. Hirsch, Sprockhövel-Hasslinghausen

District Savings Bank, Neuwied. Entrance and vestibule doors are automatic, controlled via the foot switch grid. The vestibule doors have a wide, hand-polished, stone-grey centre band for privacy. Both sets of doors have decorative, incised and polished bevel-cutting.

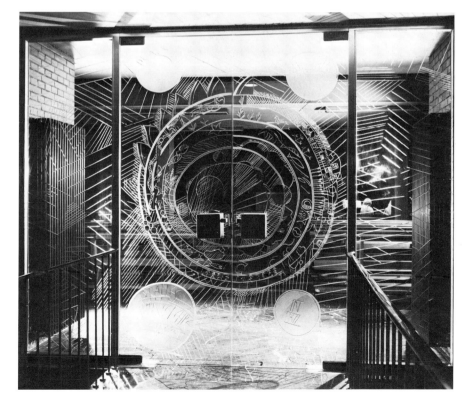

Ganzglas-Türanlage am St. Vinzenz-Krankenhaus. Karlsruhe. Keilschnittschliff auf blankem Glasgrund.

Entwurf Emil Wachter, Karlsruhe
Ausführung Werkstätte für Glasgestaltung K. Hirsch (Walter Hübner), Sprockhövel-Hasslinghausen

Fully-glazed door system at St. Vincent's Hospital, Karlsruhe. Bevel-cut decoration on plain glass ground.

Glasabschlußwände zur Wertpapier- und Anlageberatung in der Kassenhalle der Stadtsparkasse Leverkusen. Kristallspiegel- und Einscheiben-Sicherheitsglas mit eingeschliffenem Band, weiß und steingrau geschliffen, undurchsichtig.

Entwurf Bruno Spychalski, Hattingen/Ruhr
Ausführung Werkstätte für Glasgestaltung K. Hirsch, Sprockhövel-Hasslinghausen

Glass terminal wall of the stocks and shares and investment consultancy department in the banking hall of the City Savings Bank, Leverkusen. Crystal plate glass and toughened, safety glass with a ground and engraved band to give a white and stone grey, opaque finish.

Windfangtür an einem Wohnhaus. Die Ganzglaskonstruktion besteht aus Einscheiben-Sicherheitsglas. Gesamtmaß etwa 2,80 × 2,55 m; Tür 0,80 × 2,00 m. Auf die Scheiben sind von beiden Seiten geschlagene und z. T. angeschmolzene Stücke aus verschieden strukturierten und teilweise auch getönten Gläsern geklebt.

Bildhauer Max Kratz, Düsseldorf

Vestibule door in a detached house. The all-glass design has toughened safety glazing. Overall dimensions approx. 2.80 × 2.55 m; door 0.80 × 2.00 m. Curved wedges of variously textured and also partly tinted glass are attached and partly fused on to the panes on each side.

Ganzglas-Türanlage in einem Wohnhaus. Die Tür ist in Tiefätz-gravur mit Diamantritzerei mit Pflanzenmotiven geschmückt.
Entwurf und Ausführung Erwin W. Burger, Mailand

All-glass door in a residential block. The door surface is decorated with plant motifs, deep-etched with diamond scribing.

Ganzglas-Tür in einem Wohnhaus. Mattätzgravur in freier Kompo-sition.
Entwurf und Ausführung Willi Burger, Mailand

All-glass door in a residential block. Frosted, acid-etched design in free composition.

91

Eingangstür der ev. Heilandskirche, Stuttgart. Die Betonglasflügel besitzen außer einem Stahlrahmen aussteifende Eckwinkel und Armierungsstäbe, die nach Notwendigkeit in die Massivteile des Flügels eingelegt sind. Der Beton hat auf der Außenseite seine Zementhaut, auf der Innenseite erscheint er als Waschbeton.

Architekt Eberhard Hübner, Stuttgart

Entrance door to the Prot. Church of the Redeemer, Stuttgart. The glass-concrete and steel framing are stiffened with angle plates and reinforcing bars as required in the solid door areas. The external concrete has its natural cement film, the interior an exposed aggregate finish.

Ansicht und Grundriß 1:50, Schnitt 1:5

1 Armierung der Betonflügel
2 Nurglastür
3 Betontür
4 Zweischeiben-Isolierglas
5 Mineralfaserplatte
6 Stahlrohr 80/50/3 mm
7 Stahlrohr 80/40/3 mm
8 Stahlrohr 120/40/3 mm
9 kugelgelagerte Bänder
10 T-Profil 50/50 mm

Elevation and ground plan 1:50
Section 1:5

1 Reinforcement of concrete
2 All-glass door
3 Concrete door
4 Insulating glass
5 Mineral wool slab
6 Tubular steel 80/50/3 mm
7 Tubular steel 80/40/4 mm
8 Tubular steel 120/40/3 mm
9 Hinges on ball bearings
10 T-section 50/50 mm

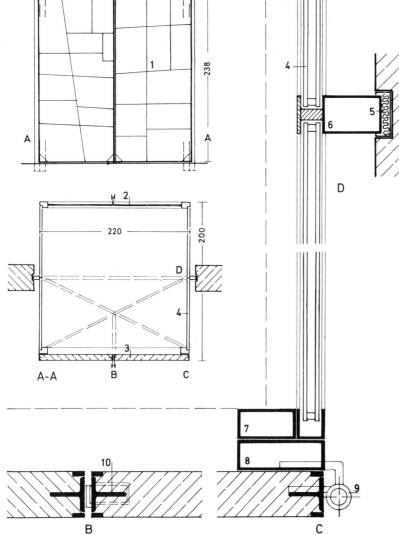

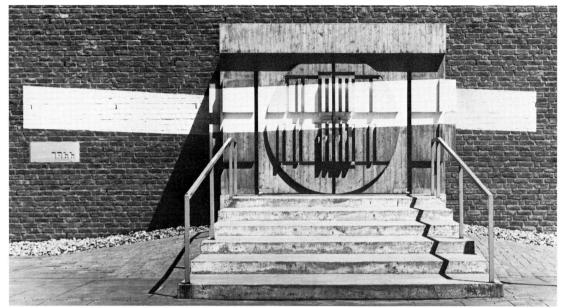

Ansicht und Grundriß 1:50
Detail 1:5

1 Verbretterung 2 mm
2 Sichtbeton-Türflügel,
  120 cm dick
3 dauerelastischer Kitt
4 Flügel, geöffnet

Elevation and ground plan 1:50
Detail 1:5

1 Casing 2 mm
2 Fair-faced concrete door leaf, 120 cm thick
3 Permanently elastic mastic
4 Leaf, opened

Heilig-Geist-Kirche, Lemgo. Vor die Kirchenwand aus Handstrichziegeln ist der Windfang aus Sichtbeton gestellt. Die zweiflügelige Eingangstür ist ebenfalls Sichtbeton. Ihr kräftiges Relief setzt sich auf den Seitenwänden des Windfangs fort. Ein weißer über Mauerwerk und Beton gezogener Streifen betont die Eingangssituation. Türanschlag mit Zapfenbändern, Bodentürschließer. Innere Windfangtüren Ganzglas.

Bildhauer Otto Herbert Hajek, Stuttgart
Architekt J. G. Hanke, Bielefeld

Church of the Holy Ghost, Lemgo. A vestibule door in fair-faced concrete has been constructed in front of the church wall of handmade bricks. The double-leaf entrance door is also in fair-faced concrete. Its powerful relief is continued in the surround. A white band extending over the doors and adjacent masonry gives emphasis to the entrance. Hanging stile with mortise hinges, floor closers. Inside fully-glazed vestibule door.

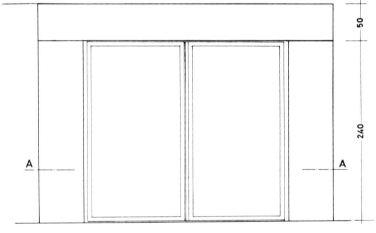

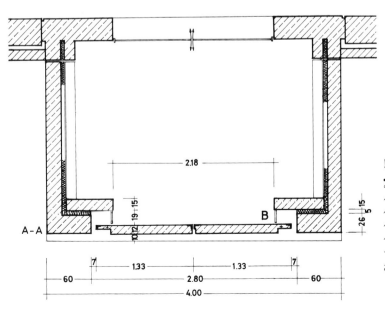

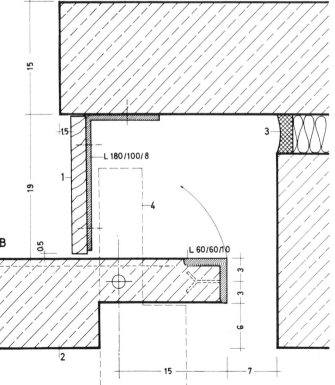

Kath. Gemeindezentrum Gaggenau, Seiteneingang. Außen- und Innenfläche der Sperrholztür sind mit wasserabstoßend imprägnier-
tem Rindsleder bezogen. Darauf sind aus rostfreiem Stahlblech aus-
geschnittene symbolische Darstellungen gelegt und angeschraubt.

Entwurf Horst Antes, Wolfartsweier bei Karlsruhe
Architekt Rainer Disse, Karlsruhe

R. Cath. church hall, Gaggenau, side entrance. The plywood door
surfaces are covered both inside and out with water-repellent
hide. Cut-out stainless steel symbolic "appliqué" designs are
superimposed on these and face-screwed.

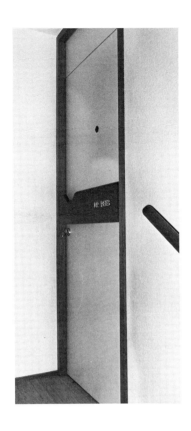

1 blockverleimte Platte 30 mm
2 Hemlock 90 × 20 mm
3 Spanplatte 10 mm
4 Messingblech 1 mm, mit Kontaktkleber befestigt und alle 5 cm aufgeschraubt
5 Messingblech 1,5 mm
6 Türgriff Ultramid schwarz
7 Spanplatte 12 mm
8 Resopal matt weiß
9 Abstandsrohre ⌀ 12 mm verchromt
10 Eiche 150 × 22 mm
11 Türband Messing
12 Kunststoffhohlprofil

1 Glued laminated block panel, 30 mm
2 Hemlock, 90 × 20 mm
3 Particle board, 10 mm
4 Brass sheet, 1 mm attached by contact adhesive and face-screwed at 5 cm intervals
5 Brass sheet, 1.5 mm
6 Door pulls in black nylon
7 Particle board, 12 mm
8 Plastic laminate facing, matt white
9 Spacer, 12 mm chrome-plated tube
10 Oak, 150 × 22 mm
11 Brass hinge
12 Hollow plastics section

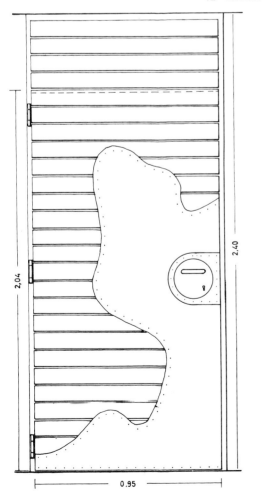

Wohnungsumbau in Karlsruhe. Die Wohnungstür ist 0,95 × 2,04 m groß und eine Holzrahmenkonstruktion, die auf der Innenseite teils mit Brettern, teils mit Messingblech bekleidet ist. Türgriff Nylon schwarz. Die Außenseite ist mit weißem Resopal belegt.

Architekt Dr.-Ing. Reinhard Gieselmann, Wien

Residential conversion, Karlsruhe. The front door, 0.95 × 2.04 m, is of wood-framed construction with interior cladding partly of boards, partly of brass sheet. Black nylon door handle. The exterior is faced with white plastic laminate.

Ansicht 1:20, Schnitt 1:5   Elevation 1:20, Section 1:5

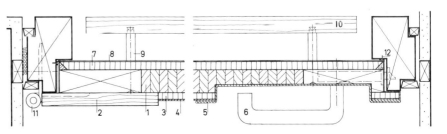

Hoteleingang in Rigi-Kaltbad/Schweiz. Türblatt und Seitenfeld sind mit altem Tornister-Leder bekleidet und mit alten Schuhnägeln beschlagen. Als Türgriff wurde eine alte geschmiedete Mausefalle verwendet, Griffstück mit Leder bezogen.

Architekt Dr.-Ing. Justus Dahinden, Zürich

Hotel entrance, Rigi-Kaltbad, Switzerland. Door leaf and side bay are covered in antique pouch leather and studded with hobnails. An old, wrought iron mouse-trap, partly covered in leather, serves as door-handle.

Portal der kath. Kirche in Langhurst/Baden. Die beiden Türflügel sind aus Eichenbohlen natur, Flügelmaß 1,08 × 2,30 m und 0,92 × 2,30 m. Zapfenlager mit Bodentürschließer. Türgriff feststehend, aus 30 mm Rundmessing geschmiedet. Geschnitzte Friese aus Eichenholz 30 cm breit, vergoldet und farbig gebeizt, mit Darstellungen aus der Apokalypse. Ganz rechts ein 25 cm breiter Streifen aus Spiegelglas 8 mm.

Bildhauer Franz Gutmann, Münstertal
Erzbischöfliches Bauamt Freiburg (Architekt Laule)

Portal of the R. Cath. Church at Langhurst, Baden. The two door wings are of natural oak boards, wing dimensions 1.08 × 2.30 m and 0.92 × 2.30 m. Mortise hinge support with floor closer. Fixed door pull, a 30 mm wrought brass ring. Carved oak frieze 30 cm wide, gilded and stained, with representations of the Apocalypse. Far right, a 25 cm strip of plate glass, 8 mm.

Eingangstür der kath. Kirche St. Martin, Jettingen. Zweiflügelige Tür, Flügelmaß etwa 1,20 × 3,00 m. Holzrahmenkonstruktion, beidseitig mit Bohlen aus dunkelbraun gebeiztem, feinjährigem Kiefernholz aufgedoppelt (Nut und Feder). Durchlaufende massive Griffleisten.

Architekt Alexander Freiherr von Branca, München

Entrance door to R. Cath. Church of St. Martin, Jettingen. Double-wing door, wing dimensions approx. 1.20 × 3.00 m. Wood-framed construction with boarding on both sides of dark brown stained, close-grained pine (tongue and groove). Continuous solid edge mouldings.

Flurtür des Kinderzimmers in einem Einfamilienhaus. Die Teilung des Türblatts ermöglicht zugfreies Lüften. Vor allem bleiben die Kleinkinder so in ihrem Bereich, jedoch mit Sicht- und Rufkontakt. Maße des Türblatts 0,75 × 2,00 m, darüber ein 50 cm hohes verglastes Oberlicht. Die beiden Türblätter können mit einem Riegel (Flurseite) verbunden werden, als Türverschluß dient der Holzdrehgriff. Holzart Eiche gewachst.
Architekten H. W. Thesing + Partner, Düsseldorf

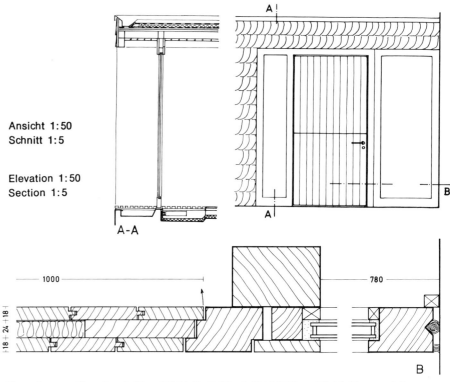

Ansicht 1:50
Schnitt 1:5

Elevation 1:50
Section 1:5

Hauseingangstür mit geteiltem Türblatt, Größe 1,10 × 2,05 m. Türblattkonstruktion aus Pitchpine: Rahmen beidseitig mit Nut- und Federbrettern 100 × 18 mm aufgedoppelt. Dazwischen Isolierung aus 20 mm Hartschaum. Außen dunkelbraun offenporig gestrichen, innen natur lasiert. Zur Verbindung der beiden Teile ein in den Griffstangen laufender Schieberiegel (Stahlprofil 15/15 mm in Rohr 20/20/2 mm). Seitliche Glasfelder 34,5 bzw. 68 cm breit, Isolierglas.   Architektin Gisela Schmidt-Krayer, Hülsenbusch

Corridor door to nursery in a private house. The "Dutch" door-leaf division permits draught-free ventilation. Above all the children have their own quarters but can be watched and are within call. Dimensions of door leaf 0.75 × 2.00 m, with a 50 cm deep, glazed fanlight. The two door leaves can be joined by a bolt (corridor side). The wooden door lever acts as lock. Waxed oak wood.

◁

Landhaus in Mitterfischen am Ammersee. Zweiteilige Tür zum Garten. Rahmenkonstruktion aus Eichenholz mit Aufdoppelung aus 18 mm Mooreiche. Koppelung der beiden Türblätter durch Magnet. Türmaß 0,99 × 2,03 m. Oberlicht aus Gußglas.

Architekt Dr.-Ing. e. h. Franz Hart, München

Country house in Mitterfischen on Lake Ammersee. 2-part ("Dutch") door to garden. Oak-framed construction with boarding of 18 mm bog-oak. Magnetic door-coupling. Door dimensions 0.99 × 2.03 m. Fanlight of cast glass.

Entrance door to house with "Dutch" divided door leaf, dimensions 1.10 × 2.05 m. Leaf construction of pitch pine: frames with tongue-and-groove boarding, 100 × 18 mm, on each side. Cavity insulation of 20 mm rigid polyurethane foam. External, open-pore paint coating in dark brown, interior natural varnish glaze. The upper and lower sections are connected by a sliding, vertical bolt in retaining straps (sectional steel 15/15 mm in tube 20/20/2 mm). Glazed bays on each side 34.5 and 68.5 cm wide respectively with insulating glass.

Eingangsportal der kath. St. Kilians-Kirche in Osterburken. Der linke Flügel ist als Gehflügel mit Zapfenbändern und Bodentürschließer angeschlagen, die mittleren Flügel mit Einsteckbändern. Flügelmaß 1,00 × 2,50 m. Unterkonstruktion Stahlrohr. Auf die Ausfachung aus Holzspanplatten sind beidseitig Eichenklötze 85/85 mm aufgeleimt und verschraubt. Sie sind 45 und 25 mm hoch, so daß ihre Vorderflächen schachbrettartig um 20 mm vor- und rückspringen. Das Eichenholz ist olivgrün lasierend gebeizt, die Schmalkanten des Türblattes und auch die Zwischenfriese sind mit Kupferblech bekleidet.

Entwurf Erzbischöfliches Bauamt Heidelberg (Architekt M. Schmitt-Fiebig, E. Eisele, A. Hafner) zusammen mit Bildhauer Emil Wachter, Karlsruhe

Entrance portal to the R. Cath. St. Killans Church, Osterburken. The left wing acts as swing access door with mortise hinges and floor closer. The centre wing has concealed hinges. Wing dimensions 1.00 × 2.50 m. Framing sub-structure of tubular steel. Oak cubes are glued and screwed onto the infilling chipboard panels on both exterior and interior. These are 45 and 25 cm deep, so that the chequered surface alternately projects or recedes by 20 mm. The oak is olive-green with varnished glaze, the narrow edge of the door leaf and the intermediary vertical bands have copper sheet cladding.

1 Eichenklötze, Hirnholz, 85 × 85 mm
2 Hartfaserplatte 19 mm
3 Rechteckstahlrohr 120/80/6 mm

1 Oak blocks, end-grain, 85 × 85 mm
2 Chipboard panel, 19 mm
3 Tubular steel, 120/80/6 mm

4 Tubular steel, 60/45/6 mm
5 Angle plate, 15/15/5 mm
6 Copper sheet, 0.5 mm

Section 1:5

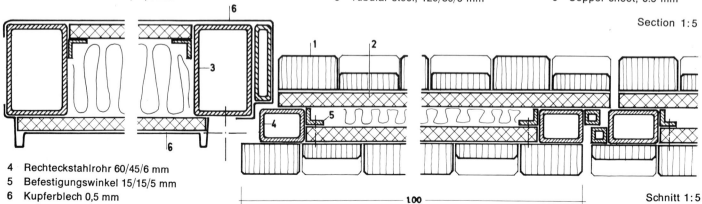

4 Rechteckstahlrohr 60/45/6 mm
5 Befestigungswinkel 15/15/5 mm
6 Kupferblech 0,5 mm

Schnitt 1:5

Eingangstür der kath. Kirche in Reutlingen-Orschelhagen. Die zwei-
flügelige Tür, Gesamtmaß 2,50 × 2,10 m, hat eine tragende Kon-
struktion aus Stahlprofilen. Die auf beiden Seiten aufgebrachte
Holzbekleidung besteht aus verleimtem Kiefern-Hirnholz 20 × 20 cm
(Seiten abgeschrägt, unterschiedlich hoch) und ist von hinten an
Stahlblechplatten geschraubt, die an dem Metallrahmen befestigt
sind. Anschlag mit Zapfenbändern. Kiefernholz natur belassen,
Stahlteile graphitgrau lackiert.
Entwurf und Ausführung Dieter Hannemann, Stuttgart
Architekt Wilfried Beck-Erlang, Stuttgart

Entrance door to the R. Cath. Church at Reutlingen-Orschelhagen.
The double-leaf door, overall dimensions 2.50 × 2.10 m, is of loadbearing, steel sectional construction. The wood cladding on both
sides consists of glued laminated pine, 20 × 20 cm (sides bevelled, of varying depth) and is screwed from behind to steel sheets
attached to the metal frame. Door stop with mortise hinges. Natural pine, steel components painted graphite grey.

Beichtstuhl in der Kirche St. Marien, Sindelfingen. Die Sperrholz-
türen, 0,98 × 2,25 m groß, sind mit 16 cm breiten Brettern aus
18 mm Buchenholz beleimt. Die Fugen zwischen den Brettern und
die Zarge sind schwarz gebeizt. Holzgriffe 16 × 16 cm. Verglasung
mit Rauchglas.
Architckt Paul Nagler, Sindelfingen

Confessional in the Church of St. Mary, Sindelfingen. The plywood
doors, 0.98 × 2.25 m, have 16 cm wide board facings of 18 mm
beechwood. The joints between the boards and the door frame
are stained black. Wooden push-pull plates, 16 × 16 cm. Glazing
with smoked glass.

Eingang zu einem Ferienhaus bei Anawyssos, Griechenland. Die Tür steht in einer 5 × 3 m großen Fensterwand, vor der ein Gitter aus Holzprofilen angebracht ist (senkrechte Stäbe 25 × 70 mm, eingelassene waagrechte Friese 25 × 80 mm). Die Tür trägt außen eine verdeckt geschraubte Aufdoppelung aus Eichenbrettern 70 × 15 mm. Die kleinen Holzflügel im feststehenden Teil des Eingangs-Elements können ganz aus dem Rahmen entfernt werden (Lüftung). Das Holzgitter vor dem Rahmen sichert dann die Öffnungen.

Architekt G. A. Skiadaressis, Athen

Entrance to a holiday residence near Anawyssos, Greece. The door is set in a 5 × 3 m window-wall with a timber grille (vertical slats 25 × 70 mm, with horizontal bands inserted, 25 × 80 mm) in front. The door has external oak boarding, 70 × 15 mm, with concealed face-screws. The small wooden wings in the fixed part of the entrance unit are completely removable (for ventilation). The openings are protected by the timber grille.

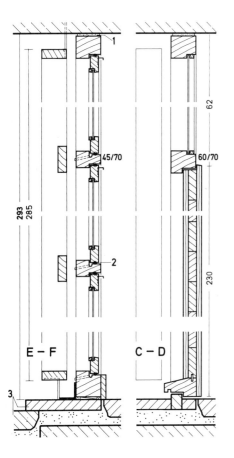

Schnitte 1:10

1 dauerelastischer Kitt
2 Kugelschnäpper
3 Marmor

Sections 1:10

1 Permanently elastic mastic
2 Bullet catch
3 Marble

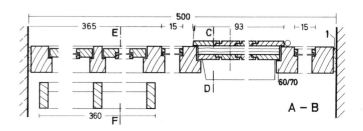

Tür im Sockelgeschoß eines Wohnhauses. Sie führt vom Wohnraum zum Garten. Blendrahmentür aus Pitchpine, 0,97 × 1,67 m. Auf den Türrahmen sind außen schmale Bretter mit 1 cm Abstand aufgeschraubt. Das dahinterliegende geschlossene Blatt (furnierte Tischlerplatte) kann zum Lüften geöffnet werden. Auf Fensterlüftung wurde verzichtet, um das Eindringen von Mäusen und anderen Tieren aus dem nahe liegenden Wald zu verhindern.

Architektin Gisela Schmidt-Krayer, Hülsenbusch

Basement door in the mezzanine of a private house, leading from the living-room to the garden. Pitch pine door casing 0.97 × 1.67 m. Narrow boards are screwed externally to the door framing at 1 cm intervals. The closed leaf behind (veneered coreboard) may be opened for ventilation. There is no window ventilation to prevent entry of mice and other animals from the adjacent forest.

Schule am Staudenbühl, Zürich. Die Rahmentüren sind mit 18 mm Kiefernholzbrettern aufgedoppelt. Die Auflage aus 2 mm Stahlblech ist aufgeschraubt und farbig lackiert.
Architekt Rolf Keller, Zürich

School at the Staudenbuehl, Zurich. The framed doors have 18 mm pine board facings. The decorative appliqué design is in 2 mm sheet steel, screwed on and painted. It represents Swiss proverbs.

Schiebe-Falttür zwischen Eingangshalle und Sitzungssaal im Rathaus Bönnigheim. In der siebenteiligen Wand, 7,00 × 2,75 m groß, sind zwei Gehflügel eingesetzt. Die sieben aus Holz gearbeiteten Platten laufen oben in einer Metallführungsschiene. Bemalung mit Lackfarben. Auf der Innenseite ist die Wand blau/rot.

Maler Karl Pfahler, Fellbach bei Stuttgart
Architekt Roland Ostertag, Stuttgart

Sliding folding door between the entrance hall and Council Chamber in the Town Hall, Boennigheim. The 7-unit wall, 7.00 × 2.75 m in area, has 2 swing access doors, each 1 unit wide. The seven wooden panels run on overhead guide rails. Artistic finish in lacquered colours. Interior wall blue and red.

Gesamtschule Osterburken. Trennwand zwischen Bühne (Mehrzweckraum) und Zuschauerraum (Eingangshalle). Die beiden Schiebeflügel, je 3,60 × 3,20 m, sind aus Tischlerplatten hergestellt und farbig lackiert. Im rechten Flügel eine Schlupftür 1,00 × 2,05 m. Türanschlag Stahlprofile mit Holzbekleidung, weiß lackiert.

Entwurf der Türen Siegfried Kischko, Berlin
Architekten J. Bassenge, K. Puhan-Schulz, H. Schreck, Berlin

Comprehensive school, Osterburken. Partition between stage (multi-purpose area) and auditorium (entrance hall). The two sliding wings, each 3.60 × 3.20 m are of coreboard, with coloured lacquer finish. In the R. H. wing is a wicket door, 1.00 × 2.05 m. Door stiles sectional steel with wood cladding, painted white.

Gesamtschule in Stuttgart-Neugereut. Ein Teil der Eingangshalle ist in Art eines Amphitheaters stufenweise abgesenkt; die Stufen führen weiter in den ein Geschoß tiefer liegenden Musiksaal. Eine Faltschiebewand von ca. 15 × 3 m trennt beide Bereiche. Ihre Tafeln, 1,20 × 3,06 m groß, sind mittig aufgehängt, paarweise miteinander verbunden und können geöffnet seitlich verschoben werden. Die Metall-Holz-Konstruktion ist 8 cm dick. Die Platten sind seitlich durch Nuten und Gummidichtungen verbunden, oben und unten sorgen je 6 Lippendichtungen für Schalldichtheit. Auf die Türfelder sind auf der Hallenseite 12 mm Sperrholzplatten geschraubt, die gespachtelt, grundiert und mit Akrylfarben bemalt sind.

Maler Lude Döring, Gutenberg (Württ.)
Architekten B. Perlia, W. Schliebitz, J. Schwarz, Stuttgart

Comprehensive school at Stuttgart-Neugereut. Part of the entrance hall is in the form of a sunken amphitheatre. The steps lead down to a music room 1 storey below. A folding, sliding partition wall, approx. 15 × 3 m, separates the two areas. The panels, 1.20 × 3.06 m in area, are hung centrally, in pairs, and can be pushed back to the side when open. The metal-wood construction system is 8 cm thick. The panels have tongue-and-groove side joints and rubber sealing strips. Above and below lipped strips provide sound-proofing. On the hall side, 12 mm plywood panels are face-screwed on to the door bays. These are filled, planed, primed and coated with acrylic paint.

Ev. Kirche in Stuttgart-Untertürkheim. Die sechsteilige Schiebewand unterteilt das Kirchenschiff in Gemeindesaal und Gottesdienstraum. Auf die Holzkonstruktion sind auf der Seite des Kirchenraumes 5 mm dicke Aluminiumbleche aufgeschraubt. Diese 36 Felder sind mit Japanpapier bezogen, auf die HAP Grieshaber Szenen aus der Josephs-Legende im Holzschnitt gedruckt hat.

Entwurf und Ausführung HAP Grieshaber, Reutlingen-Achalm

Architekten des Umbaus Karl Elsässer, Rolf Keller und Annemarie Keller-Elsässer

Prot. Church, Stuttgart-Untertuerkheim. The 6-part sliding wall separates the nave into church hall and place of worship. Facing the latter, 5 mm thick aluminium sheet is screwed on to the wood core system. These 36 bays are covered in Japan paper on which scenes from the Legend of Joseph are printed in woodcut.

1 Aluminiumblech 5 mm, 145 × 122 cm
2 Japanpapier, aufkaschiert
3 Tür zum Stapelraum für die aufgeschobenen Wandteile
4 Aluminium 10 mm

1 Aluminium sheet 5 mm, 145 × 122 cm
2 Japan paper, laminated
3 Door to stacking area for the sliding panels
4 Aluminium, 10 mm

Schnitte 1:5
Sections 1:5

Altenheim Hersbruck bei Nürnberg. Die Türflügel zum Speisesaal sind 0,95 × 2,00 m groß, Raumhöhe 2,60 m. Sie bestehen, ebenso wie der feststehende Teil darüber aus einer 30 mm dicken Tischlerplatte. Sie ist beidseitig mit Resopal überzogen, dessen Dekorpapier individuell gestaltet ist. Die Türen sind Bestandteil einer farbigen Raumgestaltung.

Maler Diether F. Domes, Langenargen
Architekten Kappler & Nützel, Nürnberg

Old people's home, Hersbruck near Nuremberg. The door wings to the dining-room measure 0.95 × 2.00 m, 2.60 m room height. Wings and fixed transom are of 30 mm thick coreboard slabs, coated on both sides with plastic laminate, with individually designed, decorative paper ground. The doors form an integral component of the colour scheme of the room.

Klassenzimmertüren in der Realschule Kreßbronn. Die Sperrholztüren, 2,00 × 1,00 m, sind mit Resopalplatten furniert, deren Dekorpapier handbemalt ist.

Maler Diether F. Domes, Langenargen
Architekt Eugen Benninger, Friedrichshafen

Classroom doors in the Secondary School, Kressbronn. The plywood doors, 2.00 × 1.00 m, are veneered with plastic laminate panels of which the paper ground is hand-painted.

Gesamtschule Osterburken. Die Türen zu den naturwissenschaftlichen Fachräumen sind mit Resopal furnierte Tischlerplatten. Blattgröße 1,00 × 2,10 m. Stahlzarge mit Moosgummidichtung. Das Dekorpapier der Schichtstoffplatten trägt stilisierte, fachbezogene Darstellungen.

Entwurf der Türen Siegfried Kischko, Berlin
Architekten J. Bassenge, K. Puhan-Schulz, H. Schreck, Berlin

Comprehensive School, Osterburken. The doors to the science laboratories are of coreboard with plastic laminate veneer. Leaf dimensions 1.00 × 2.10 m. Steel door casing with foam rubber sealing. The decorative paper of the plastics panels has stylized motifs relating to the subjects studied.

Einfamilienhaus bei Stuttgart. Die Sperrholz-Türblätter sind im Siebdruck mit Polyesterlack beschichtet und anschließend mit mattem Klarlack gespritzt.
Entwurf Heinz Herold, Stuttgart
Architekten Kammerer + Belz, Stuttgart

Private house near Stuttgart. The plywood door leaves have a screen-print, polyester paint coating, sprayed with clear varnish.

Turnhalle der Hardtschule, Weilheim/
Obb. Die Türen an der Längsseite der
Halle sind teils als Schwingtore, teils als
Flügeltüren ausgebildet. Es sind Holz-
türen, die auf dunkelblauem Grund
große weiße Buchstaben tragen: G =
Geräte, E = Eingangsraum.

Entwurf Manfred Mayerle und Andreas
Sobeck, München

Architekt Kurt Ackermann, München

Gymnasium of the Hard School, Weil-
heim/Upper Bavaria. The doors on the
long side of the hall are partly of swing
and partly of double-wing design. They
are of wood, with white, door-high lettering on a dark blue ground: G =
equipment (Geraete), E = entrance.

Kindertagesheim in Hamburg-Stellingen. Hier wurden 26 Sperrholz-türen verschiedener Größe mit Resopalplatten furniert, deren De-korpapier aus verschieden gefärbten Stücken zusammengesetzt sind. Die Türen im Bild rechts tragen (von links) folgende Farben: Grün-Weiß-Grün mit blauem Punkt, Grün-Blau-Rot, Orange und Rot auf Weiß.

Entwurf Maria Pirwitz, Hamburg · Architekt S. Wolske, Hamburg

Day nursery, Hamburg-Stellingen. Here 26 plywood doors of various sizes have plastic laminate ground veneering, of which the decorative paper is composed of abstract shapes in different colours. The doors shown (right) have the following colours (from L. to R.) green-white-green with blue spot, green-blue-red, orange and red on white.

◁   ▷

Kath. Kindergarten Markdorf. Abgesperrte Türblätter, beidseitig mit Resopal furniert. Für die Flurseiten wurden die Dekorpapiere individuell gestaltet, für die Raumseite se-rienmäßige Platten verwendet.

Entwurf Roland Peter Litzenburg, Leimbach

R. Cath. Kindergarten, Markdorf. Flush door leaves, plastic laminate veneered on both sides. The decorative paper was indi-vidually designed for the corridor side; for the room-side, serially-produced sheets were used.

Gesamtschule an der Freudstraße, München. Die Tür zum Musiksaal trägt die Buchstaben MU in ihrer Resopalbekleidung. Entsprechend sind die anderen Sonderklassen mit BI (Biologie), CH (Chemie) usw. gekennzeichnet.

Entwurf der Türen Manfred Mayerle und Andreas Sobeck, München   Architekt Erhard Fischer, München

Comprehensive school in Freudstrasse, Munich. The door to the Music Room incorporates the letters MU in the plastic laminate cladding. The other special classrooms are correspondingly designated BI (Biology), CH (Chemistry) etc.

Gästekasino der Firma Siemens AG, München. Die Flurtür, ein handelsübliches abgesperrtes Türblatt, ist beidseitig mit blau-weiß gestreiftem Formica belegt und weist dadurch auf den Kasinoraum hin, der in denselben Farben gehalten ist (Bild unten).

Architekt Hans Hollein, Wien

Visitors' canteen for the Siemens AG Company, Munich. The corridor door, a proprietary, cross-banded door leaf, is covered on both sides with blue-and-white striped formica and thus relates to the canteen itself which has the same colour scheme (see Photo below).

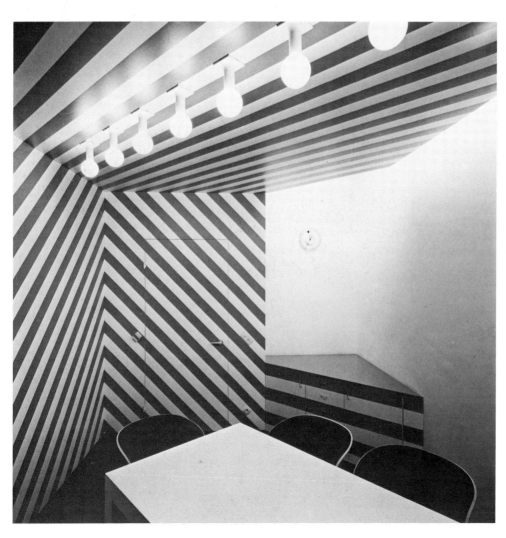

Die Türen im Krematorium Leinfelden nehmen die Kreuzform der zweiflügeligen Außentüren (vergl. S. 85) auf. Es sind Vollspantüren, auf die die „halbe Kreuzform" entweder durch die aufgedoppelten, mit DD-Lack verschiedenfarbig gestrichenen Spanplatten bewirkt wird oder durch die Griffstange aus rostfreiem Stahlrohr ϕ 20 mm.

oben: Empfang. Rahmen von Schalter und Türblatt purpurrot, Zierteil des Türblattes ultramarinblau.

unten: Warteraum. Türblatt ultramarinblau, Türzarge purpurrot.

Architekten Max Bächer und Harry G. H. Lie, Stuttgart

The doors to the Leinfelden Crematorium assume the cruciform of the double-wing external doors (cf. p. 85). They are full-span doors on which the „half-cross" motif appears either in the faced coreboard panels, painted in different colours or in the contour of the stainless steel tube, dia. 20 mm forming the door pull and extending round the door leaf.

Above: Reception counter and door leaf purple, decorative door element ultramarine.

Below: Waiting room. Door leaf ultramarine, door casing purple.

Einfamilienhaus mit Zahnarzt-Praxis in Metzingen. Der Windfang ist eine Bohlenkonstruktion, mit wetterfestem Sperrholz bekleidet und leuchtend gelb lakkiert. Eingangstür Holzrahmen, beidseitig mit Sperrholz bekleidet. Zweischeiben-Isolierglas. Klingelplatte und Briefkasten-Abdeckung Aluminium dunkelbronze eloxiert.

Architekten Dolmetsch + Haug, Metzingen

Detached house with dentist's practice, Metzingen. The vestibule is of boarded construction, with weatherproof, plywood cladding, painted bright yellow. Entrance door timber-framed, with plywood cladding on each side. 2-ply insulating glass. Bell-plate and letter-plate of anodized, dark bronze aluminium.

Grundriß und Schnitt 1:20

1 Eingangstür
2 Tür zur Wohnung
3 Tür zur Praxis
4 Briefkasten
5 Isolierglas
6 Lichtschacht

Ground plan and section 1:20

1 Entrance door
2 Door to house
3 Door to practice
4 Letter-boxes
5 Insulating glass
6 Light well

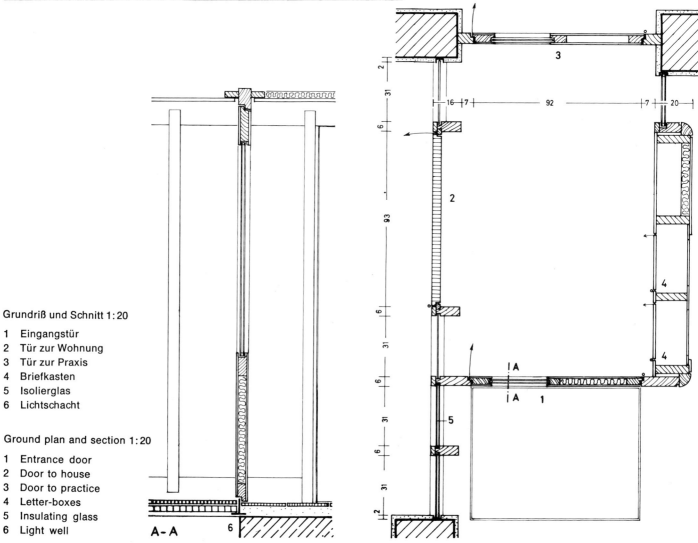

Regional Law Courts, Mannheim. Entrance to Sessions Hall of the Civil Chamber. Double-leaf door, approx. 1.00 × 2.20 m. Sub-structure wood, with superimposed, hand-moulded shells of glass-fibre reinforced polyester joined at the edges to the framing. The door handles follow the curvature of these shells. Door stop with floor closer, dark anodized frame. In the lower door frame a hollow, sound-absorbent chamber is substituted for the door sill. Fanlight with sheet glass panels.

R. Cath. Church for the Furt Valley, Regensdorf, Switzerland. The access doors to the hall of worship are double-wing, wooden doors (of composite construction) with leaf dimensions of 1.25 × 2.25 m. The overhead panelling measures 2.25 × 1.35 m. The wood surfaces are painted dark blue. The decorative edging of stainless steel is glued on to the swing door. Door plate also of stainless steel.

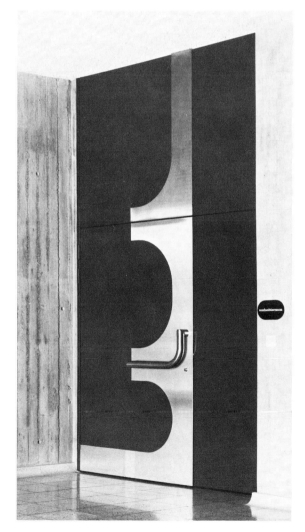

Landgericht Mannheim. Eingang zum Sitzungssaal der Zivilkammer. Zweiflügelige Tür, etwa 1,00 × 2,20 m. Unterkonstruktion Holz. Darauf auf beiden Seiten handgeformte Schalen aus glasfaserverstärktem Polyester, die an den Kanten mit der Unterkonstruktion verbunden sind. Die Türgriffe sind an diese Schalen angeformt. Anschlag mit Bodentürschließer an die dunkel eloxierte Rahmenkonstruktion. Statt eines unteren Türanschlags wurde in den unteren Türrahmen eine Schallschluckkammer eingebaut. Oberlicht mit Rohglasfüllung.

Architekt Helmut Striffler, Mannheim

Kath. Pfarreizentrum für das Furttal, Regensdorf/Schweiz. Die Zugänge zum Andachtsraum sind zweiflügelige Holztüren (Verbundkonstruktion) mit einem Flügelmaß von 1,25 × 2,25 m. Die Füllung über den Flügeln ist 2,25 × 1,35 m groß. Die Holzflächen sind tiefblau lackiert; die Zierblende auf dem Gehflügel ist rostfreier Stahl, aufgeklebt. Griffstange ebenfalls rostfreier Stahl.

Architekten Huber + Trachsel, Zürich

Klassenzimmertür im Gymnasium Locarno. Türblatt aus Fichte, mit schmalen senkrechten Brettern aufgedoppelt, weiß lackiert. Die blaue 3 ist Teil einer den ganzen Raum umfassenden Malerei von Livio Bernasconi, Carona.

Architekt Dolf Schnebli, Agno/Schweiz

Classroom door Secondary School, Locarno. Door leaf of spruce with narrow, vertical boarding, painted white. The "3" in blue forms part of the room decoration scheme by Livio Bernasconi, Carona.

Schnitt 1:5

1 Spanplatte 28 mm
2 Magnetschnäpper
3 Putzschiene Protektor

Section 1:5

1 Particle board, 28 mm
2 Magnetic catch
3 Plaster track

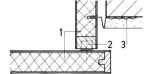

Gesamtschule an der Freudstraße, München. Flurtür des Umkleideraums der ärztlichen Untersuchungsstelle. Tür und Türfutter sind gelb gestrichen.

Entwurf der Türen Andreas Sobeck und Manfred Mayerle, München · Architekt Erhard Fischer, München

Comprehensive school in Freudstrasse, Munich. Corridor door to the changing room for the medical examination station. Door and door lining painted yellow.

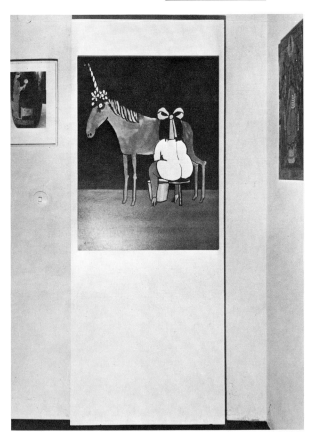

Keller in einem Einfamilienhaus. Türblatt 28 mm Spanplatte, beidseitig mit Resopal furniert, stumpf auf die Zarge schlagend. Der seitliche Überstand verdeckt die Bänder und dient als Griffleiste. Auf der Innenseite ist eine Lederschlaufe als Griff angebracht, vgl. Seite 138.

Architekt Otto Steinhöfel, Hankensbüttel

Basement in a private house. Door leaf of 28 mm particle board, veneered on both surfaces with plastic laminate. Closing butt to the door frame. The edge projection conceals the hinges and serves as a door pull moulding. On the inside a leather loop acts as door-handle (cf. p. 138).

Eingangstür zu einem Wohnhaus in Bensheim. Auf die Sperrholztür ist ein kräftiges Relief aus Holzleisten gesetzt, das auch den Türgriff mit einbezieht. Tür weiß lakkiert. Sichtbetonunterzug des Vordachs, Dreiecksfelder und Wandstreifen leuchtend blau gestrichen.

Entwurf Otto Herbert Hajek, Stuttgart

Entrance door to a detached house at Bensheim. The plywood door has a bold geometrical relief formed of wood strips, incorporating the door pull. Door painted white. Canopy with fair-faced concrete joist, triangular bays and wall strips painted bright blue.

Einfamilienhaus in Dänemark. Auf die Sperrholztüren sind ungesäumte, gehobelte Bretter aus Fichtenholz genagelt. Türblatt und Rahmen rot lackiert, rote Kunststoff-Türgriffe.

Detached house, Denmark. The plywood doors have nailed boarding with non-trimmed, waney edges of spruce. Door leaf and frame painted red, red plastics door handle.

Erweiterung der Kirche St. Martin, Meckenhausen. Neben der Eingangstür liegt der aus dem Kirchenraum herausgebaute Beichtstuhl unter einem gemeinsamen Vordach. Tür und Wandflächen sind im Aufbau und in den kreuzförmigen Aussteifungshölzern gleich. Holzwerk Fichte, mit Xylamon farblos imprägniert. Bänder, Griffplatten und Türriegel nach Entwurf geschmiedet; alle Metallteile feuerverzinkt.

Architekt Christoph Hackelsberger, München-Solln

Extension to the Church of St. Martin, Meckenhausen. The confessional has been built next to the entrance door, as an extension of the nave, with a joint canopy. Door and wall surfaces are of identical design with diagonal, timber bracing in each case. Wood structure of spruce, impregnated with transparent fungicidal, synthetic paint. Hinges, push-plates and bolts forged to the architect's design; all metal components hot-dip galvanized.

Schnitt 1:10

1 Schalung 24 mm, Nut und Feder
2 Isolierung 50 mm
3 1 Lage 500er Pappe
4 vorgesetzte Rahmen 100 × 80 mm

Section 1:10

1 Boarding 24 mm, tongue-and-groove
2 Insulation, 50 mm
3 1 layer 500-ply roofing felt
4 Frames set forward, 100 × 80 mm

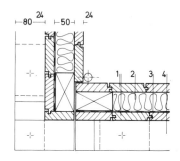

Schiebetür im ev. August-Winnig-Haus in Wilhelmsfeld bei Heidelberg. Die Tür aus Lärchenholz natur mißt 2,25 × 3,00 m. Sie läuft als Hängekonstruktion in einer Stahlschiene. Künstlerische Gestaltung durch 960 aufgeleimte Holzformen. Die Tür trennt den Andachtsraum von der Versammlungshalle.

Entwurf Peter Dreher, Freiburg
Ev. Kirchenbauamt Baden (Architekt H. Hampe †)

Sliding door in Prot. August-Winnig House, Wilhelmsfeld near Heidelberg. The door is of natural larch, measuring 2.25 × 3.00 m. It is hung on overhead steel rails. An artistic design of 960 wood disc units glued to the surface. The door separates the assembly hall from the place of worship.

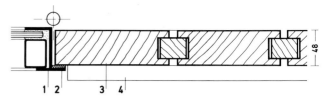

Einfamilienhaus in Holland. Das Türblatt ist mit 0,85 × 2,35 m fast raumhoch. Es besteht aus massivem Teakholz 47 mm; der Rahmen ist gestemmt, die Füllungsbretter sind durch 26 mm dicke massive Federn verbunden, Fugenbreite 10 mm. Das Türfeld ist eine Stahlkonstruktion, die mit schwarz eloxiertem Leichtmetall bekleidet und mit Drahtglas ausgefüllt ist.

Architekt Dirk van Sliedregt, Amsterdam

Private house, Holland. The door leaf of 47 mm solid teak is almost room-high, measuring 0.85 × 2.35 m. The frame is mortise rebated. The boarded panels are joined by 26 mm thick tongue-and-grooving, joint width 10 mm. The side bays are steel-framed with black, anodized cladding of light metal and wired glass panels.

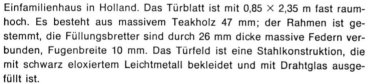

Zimmertür in einem Einfamilienhaus aus Eiche massiv.

Architekt Hans Haas, Aachen

Living-room door of solid oak, in a private house.

Windfangtür der Kirche St. Joseph in Wels-Pernau. Zweiflügelige Dreifüllungstür aus massivem, natur belassenem Fichtenholz. Jedes Türblatt mißt 1,36 × 2,96 m; Rahmenstärke 60 mm. Die Füllungsbretter sind 20 mm dick, Füllungen zweischalig mit einer Zwischenlage aus 20 mm Styropor. Über der Tür ein Gitter aus Fichtenbohlen, Zwischenfelder verglast.

Architekten Franz Riepl und Othmar Sackmauer, München

Vestibule door, Church of St. Joseph, Wels-Pernau. Double-leaf, 3-panel door of solid spruce wood left stripped. Door leaf dimensions 1.36 × 2.96 m, frame thickness 60 mm. The panel boarding is 20 mm thick, the panels are double-skin with interlining of foamed polystyrene. Over the door is a deep grille of spruce blocks with narrow glazing bays.

1 Mauerwerk
2 3maliger Schutzanstrich gegen Pilz- und Insektenbefall
3 Thiokol-Fugenverschluß
4 gerolltes Messingband 160 mm
5 Messingschraube M 8 + Messing-Beilagscheiben
6 Messing-Hutmutter
7 Styropor-Einlage
8 Ziegelplatten
9 Mörtelbett

1 Masonry
2 3 coats of paint as protection against fungi and insects
3 "Thiokol" joint sealer
4 Rolled brass strip, 160 mm
5 Brass screws, brass cover plates
6 Brass cap nuts
7 Polystyrene ply
8 Clay tiles
9 Mortar bed

Ansicht 1:50   Elevation 1:50
Schnitt 1:20   Section 1:20
Schnitte 1:5   Sections 1:5

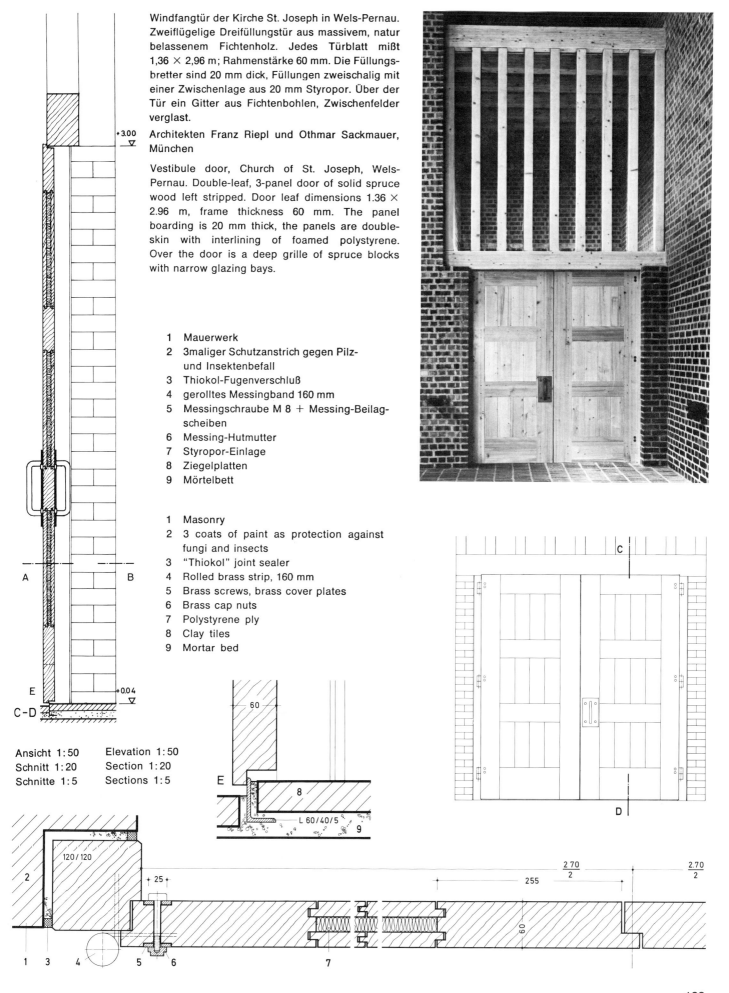

Sakristeitüren in der Kirche zum Verklärten Christus, Bad Driburg. Die rechte Tür ist aus Eiche furniert, die linke mit massiven Leisten aufgedoppelt.

Architekt Hans Haas, Aachen

Sacristy doors in the Church of Christ's Transfiguration, Bad Driburg. The R. H. door is of veneered oak, the L. H. door with panel edge mouldings.

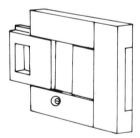

Türverschluß
Door bolt

Tür an der katholischen Kirche in Chur. Sie gleicht in der Konstruktion der Tür auf der Seite gegenüber. Hölzerne Verriegelung, die mit einem Zylinderschloß abgesperrt werden kann.

Architekten Walter M. Förderer + Ass., Schaffhausen/Schweiz

Door to the R. Cath. Church, Chur. It resembles the door opposite. Wooden bolt which can be secured with a cylindrical lock.

Kath. Kirche in Bettlach/Schweiz. Zweiflügelige Tür aus Eiche massiv. Gestemmter Rahmen, beidseitig mit Eichenriemen 100 × 18 mm bekleidet. Verschluß durch einen Holzschieberiegel auf der Innenseite. Anschlag mit Zapfenbändern, unteres Türlager auf Wandvorsprung 40 cm über Fußboden.

Architekten Walter M. Förderer + Ass., Schaffhausen/Schweiz

R. Cath. Church, Bettlach, Switzerland. Double-wing door of solid oak. Mortised frames, with oak strip cladding on both sides, 100 × 18 mm. Fastened by a sliding wooden bolt on the inside. Stop with mortise hinges, lower door supported on a wall projection extending 40 cm over the floor.

Schnitt 1:5

1 Eiche 18 mm
2 Steinwolle 16 mm
3 Rahmenhölzer 200 × 60 mm

Section 1:5

1 Oak, 18 mm
2 Rock wool, 16 mm
3 Timber framing components 200 × 60 mm

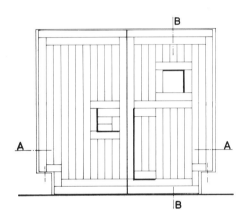

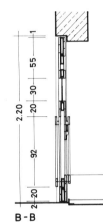

B - B

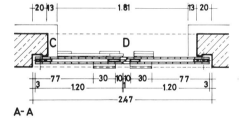

A- A

Ansicht, Grundriß
und Schnitt 1:50

Elevation, ground plan
and section 1:50

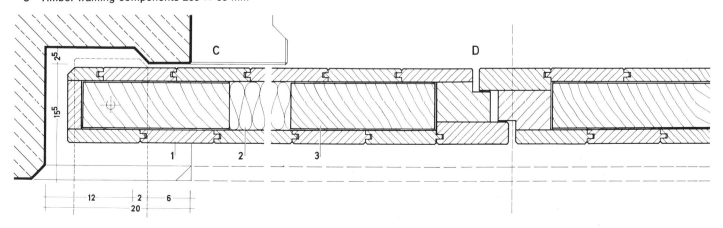

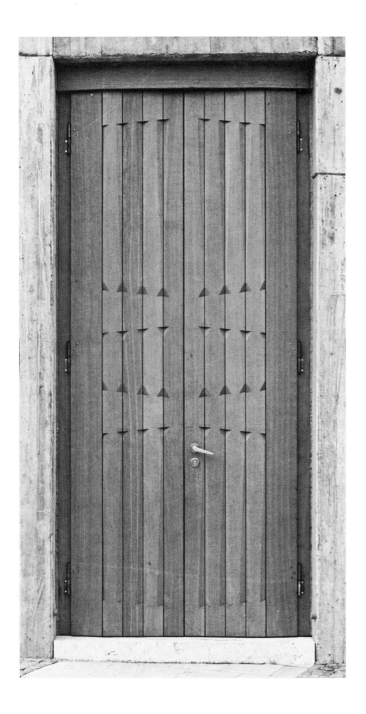

▷

1 Pivot hinge
2 Particle board with matt, red, plastic laminate veneer
3 Veneered and black stained door edging
4 Particle board, teak veneered
5 Plinth, 1 mm PVC, dark grey
6 Rigid castors, loadbearing capacity per castor 200 kg
7 Strut for load transfer to castors
8 Deck board suspended for inspection of castors
9 Cast steel plate, 10 mm
10 Position of door when open
11 Terrazzo tiles
12 Plywood, 8 mm

Kath. Kirche St. Pius, Lippstadt. Brettertür aus Eiche natur. Die Nutung auf der Außenseite nimmt die Form der inneren Friese auf.
Architekt Hans Haas, Aachen

R. Cath. Church of St. Pius, Lippstadt. Natural oak boarded doors. The external notching follows the contours of the banding on the inside.

126

Mensa der Technischen Universität, Braunschweig. Von der Eingangshalle im Erdgeschoß führt eine 2,35 × 2,29 m große Tür in den Großen Saal. Sie ist so entworfen, daß bei geschlossener Tür die Wand durchzulaufen scheint (Foto unten).

Architekt Dr.-Ing. Walter Henn, Braunschweig

Dining Hall of the Technical University, Braunschweig. A door, 2.35 × 2.29 m, leads from the entrance hall on the ground floor to the Assembly Hall. It is designed to create the impression of a continuous wall when the door is closed (see Photo below).

1 Türdrehzapfen
2 Spanplatte mit matt-rotem Resopalbelag
3 Holzleiste furniert und schwarz gebeizt
4 Spanplatte teak-furniert
5 Sockel 1 mm PVC-Belag, dunkelgrau
6 Bockrollen, Tragkraft je Rolle 200 kg
7 Streben zur Übertragung des Türgewichts auf das Bockrollenpaar
8 Deckbrett, wird zur Inspektion der Bockrollen ausgehängt
9 Stahlgußplatte 10 mm
10 Lage der geöffneten Tür
11 Kunststein-Bodenplatten
12 Sperrholz 8 mm

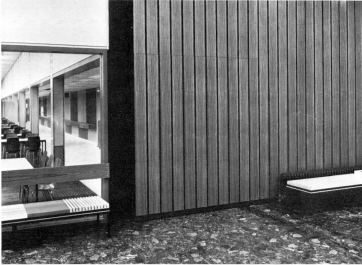

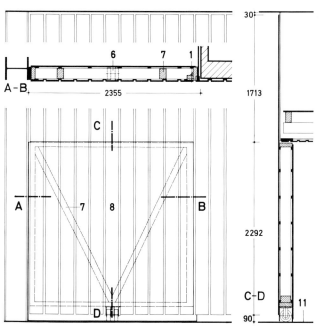

Ansicht und Schnitte 1:50
Schnitte 1:5

Elevation and sections 1:50
Sections 1:5

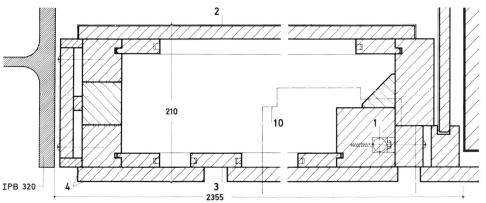

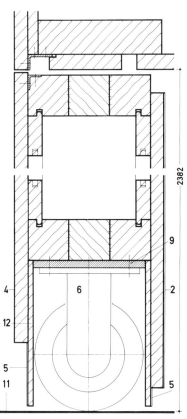

Haupteingang der Bullinger-Kirche, Zürich. Zweiflügelige aufgedoppelte Tür aus geöltem Teakholz. Türgriffe aus Messing.

Entwurf F. Maurer, Zürich
Architekten Gebrüder Pfister, Zürich

Main entrance to the Bullinger Church, Zurich. Double-wing, boarded door of oiled teak. Brass door handle.

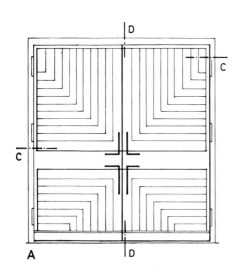

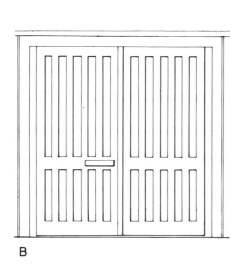

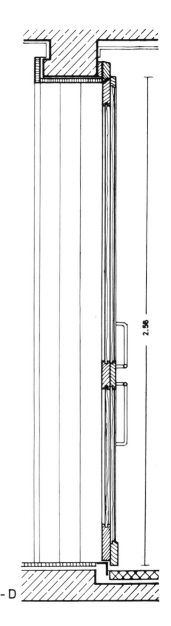

| Ansichten 1:50 | 1 Außenseite 100 × 25 mm Teak |
| Schnitte 1:20 | 2 Innenseite 100 × 44 mm und 100 × 25 mm im Wechsel |

| Elevations 1:50 | 1 Exterior, 100 × 25 mm teak |
| Sections 1:20 | 2 Interior, 100 × 44 mm and 100 × 25 mm alternating |

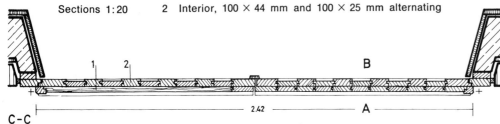

Eingangstor zur Werkstatt. Zweiflügeliges Tor mit Oberlicht. Rahmenkonstruktion aus Fichte 120 × 110 mm, offenporig dunkel gestrichen. Gesamtmaß 2,88 × 3,25 m, Flügelmaß 1,40 × 2,20 m. In jeden Flügel sind zwei Tafeln aus kräftig profiliertem, grünlichem Schmelzglas eingesetzt, Größe etwa 0,58 × 2,16 m; sie laufen jeweils hinter den horizontalen Sprossen durch. Türverschluß durch verschließbaren Treibriegel am Gehflügel.

Entwurf und Ausführung Glas + Form, Florian Lechner, Neubeuern

Entrance gate to the workshop. Double-wing gate with fanlight. Spruce frame design, 120 × 110 mm, painted dark green. Overall dimensions 2.88 × 3.25 m, wing dimensions 1.40 × 2.20 m. 2 panels of boldly profiled, green glass are set in each wing, approx. 0.58 × 2.16 m, running behind the glazing bars. Lockable cremorne bolt on access wing.

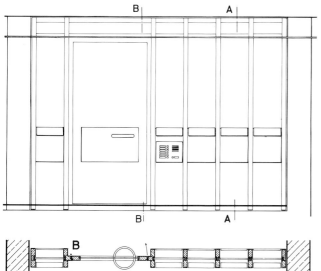

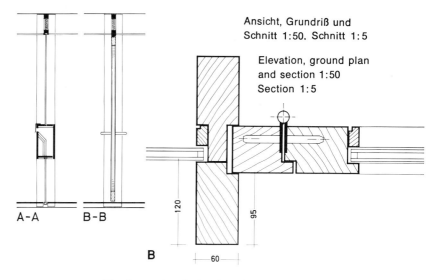

Ansicht, Grundriß und Schnitt 1:50. Schnitt 1:5

Elevation, ground plan and section 1:50 Section 1:5

Pfarrhaus des kath. Gemeindezentrums St. Josef, Stuttgart. Türblatt aus 60 mm Sperrholz, leuchtend rot lackiert. Halbkreisförmige Griffe aus Aluminiumrohr ⌀ 30 mm, im Glasfeld befestigt. Senkrechte Zargen aus Kiefernholz, offenporiger dunkelbrauner Anstrich. Klingeltafel und Briefkastendeckel Leichtmetall, dunkelbraun eloxiert; weiße Schrift. Briefkasten-Vorderseite rot lackiert. Glasfelder Zweischeiben-Sicherheitsglas.

Architekten Rainer Zinsmeister und Giselher Scheffler, Stuttgart

R. Cath. vicarage, St. Joseph's Parish, Stuttgart. Door leaf of 60 mm plywood, painted bright red. Semicircular door pull of tubular aluminium, dia. 30 mm, secured in the glass bay. Jambs of pine, painted dark brown. Bell plate and letter-plate of light alloy, anodized dark brown, with lettering in white. Letterbox front painted red. Glass panels of 2-ply, laminated safety glass.

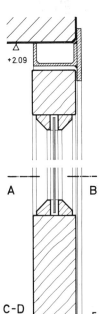

Zweiflügelige Windfangtür an der ev. Kirche in Feld-
moching. Flügelmaß 0,88 × 2,04 m. Anschlag am Rahmen aus U 60/30/4 mm. Türblatt Kiefer naturlasiert mit
Klarglasfeldern.

Architekt Johannes Ludwig, München

Double-leaf vestibule door to the Prot. Church, Feld-
moching. Wing dimensions 0.88 × 2.04 m. Stop at
frame of channelled section 60/30/4 mm. Door leaf
of natural varnished pine with clear glass panels.

Schnitte 1:5

1 Ziegelmauerwerk
2 Aufsatzband messinggerollt
3 Neoprene-Dichtungsprofil
4 Klarglas
5 Messingprofil 15/15/2 mm
6 Neoprene-Dichtungsprofil
7 Messing-Anschlagschiene 5/60 mm
8 Klinker-Flachschicht
9 Einsteckschloß, Drücker-Rosette und Drücker
   Messing
10 Türkantenriegel mit Messingabdeckplatten

Sections 1:5

1 Brick masonry
2 Cap hinge of rolled brass
3 Neoprene weatherstrip
4 Clear glass
5 Brass section
6 Neoprene weatherstrip
7 Brass door rails 5/60 mm
8 Clinker course
9 Mortise lock, rose and door latch in brass
10 Flush bolt with brass cover plates

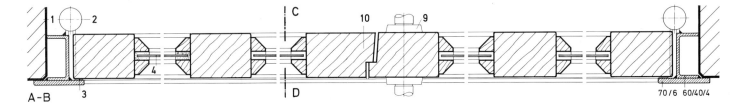

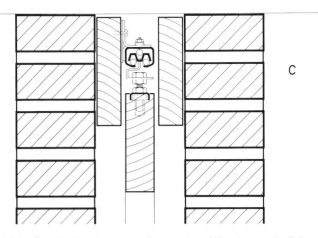

C

Schiebetür zwischen Flur und Eßraum eines Wohnhauses in Schweden. Die Schiebetüren aus Fichte natur lassen sich ganz in die Mauernischen einschieben. Auf der Flurseite ist das Sichtmauerwerk für einen großen Spiegel und eine Ablage ausgespart. Das Türblatt mißt 1,85 × 2,20 m. Rahmenhölzer 95 × 40 mm, Füllungen 17 × 40 mm mit 17 mm Abstand.

Architekten Fritz Jaenecke und Sten Samuelson, Malmö

Sliding door between hall and dining-room in a private house in Sweden. The two sliding doors of natural stripped spruce are completely retractable in the wall niches. On the hall side the exposed masonry is recessed to take a large mirror and also to form a ledge. Door leaf dimensions 1.85 × 2.20 m. Wood frame units 95 × 40 mm, panels 17 × 40 mm at 17 mm intervals.

Grundriß, Ansicht und Schnitt 1:50
Schnitte 1:5

Ground plan, elevation and section 1:50
Sections 1:5

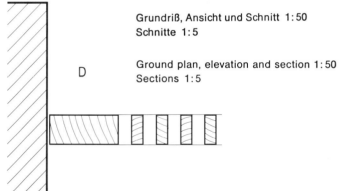

D

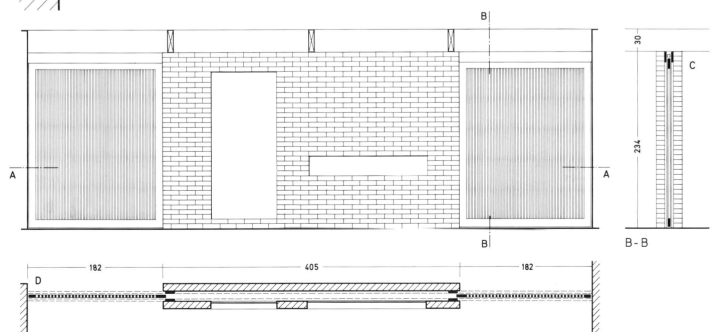

Kulturzentrum Wolfsburg, Seiteneingang. Als Hebetür angeschlagenes Blatt aus massivem, natur belassenem Afzeliaholz, streifenweise verglast.

Architekt Alvar Aalto †

Cultural Centre, Wolfsburg. Side entrance. A solid, natural afzelia wood leaf with glazing strips forms the lever gear door.

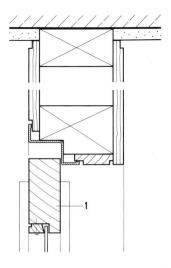

Schnitte 1:5	Sections 1:5
1 Afzelia, massiv	1 Solid afzelia
2 Sattelabdeckschiene	2 Rail cover saddle
3 Kupferblech	3 Copper sheet
4 Dachpappe	4 Roofing felt

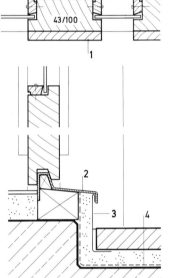

Schnitt 1:5   Section 1:5

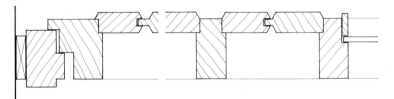

Eingangstür aus Eichenholz an einem Einfamilienhaus. Türblattgröße 0,90 × 2,05 m. Rahmen und Füllungen massiv, mit Sadolins mittelgraugrün behandelt. Glasfeld aus verschieden strukturiertem Kristallrohglas, Kanten aneinandergeklebt. Anschlag mit steigenden Bändern.

Architekt Otto Steinhöfel, Hankensbüttel

Entrance door in oak, to a private house. Door leaf dimensions 0.90 × 2.05 m. Frame and panels of solid wood, treated with medium greyish-green "Sadolins". Glass bay with crystal sheet glass of various textures, edge-glued. Stile with rising hinges.

Eingangstür des Gemeindezentrums St. Markus, Coburg. Flügelmaß 1,02 × 2,27 m. Zweifüllungstür aus Eichenholz, dunkel gebeizt. Füllungen isolierverglast und mit einem Gitter aus Eiche 65 × 25 mm hinterlegt. Auf der Außenseite ist ein dünneres Türblatt mit der gleichen Teilung aufgesetzt, es wird an jedem senkrechten Fries von vier Kupplungsschrauben (Trio-Schraube) gehalten.

Architekt Johannes Ludwig, München

Entrance door to Church Hall of St. Mark, Coburg. Wing dimensions 1.02 × 2.27 m. Two-panel door of dark, stained oak. Panels with insulating glazing backed by an oak grille, 65 × 25 mm. The exterior also has a thinner door leaf with the same divisions, attached to each vertical strip by four screw-bolt connections.

1 Insulating glass pane
2 Interchangeable sill unit, oak
3 Natural stone tile
4 "Moltoprene" sealing backing
5 "Thiokol" sealing
6 Copper sheet
7 Cremorne bolt with lever, handle and backplate
8 Screw-bolt connection
9 Floor closer

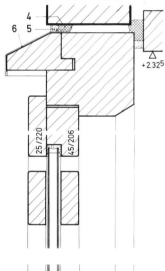

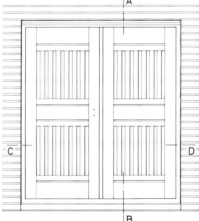

1 Isolierglasscheibe
2 auswechselbarer Schwellenteil, Eiche
3 Natursteinplatte
4 Moltopren als Dichtungsunterlage
5 Thiokol-Dichtung
6 Kupferblech
7 Treibriegel mit Hebel, Stange und Schließblech
8 Verbundschraube (Trio-Schraube)
9 Bodentürschließer

Ansicht 1:50   Elevation 1:50
Schnitte 1:5   Sections 1:5

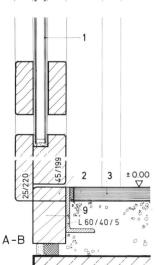

A-B

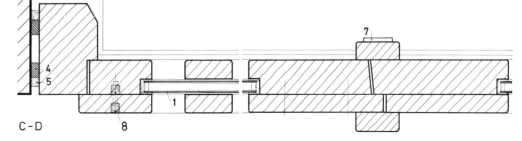

C-D

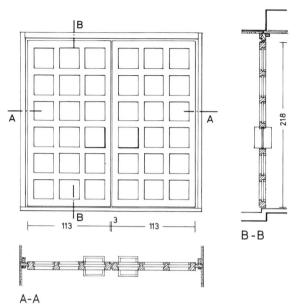

Einfamilienhaus in Stuttgart. Zweiflügelige Eingangstür aus Kiefernholz, schwarzer offenporiger Anstrich, mit Thermopane verglast. Bei den Garagentoren daneben wurde ein der Aufteilung der Haustüren entsprechendes Raster auf die Kipptorflügel aufgeschraubt.

Architekten Max Bächer und Harry G. H. Lie, Stuttgart

Private house, Stuttgart. Double-leaf entrance door of pine, with black, open-pore paint coating. "Thermopane" insulating glazing. A grid corresponding to that of the front door is screwed on to the adjacent up-and-over garage doors.

B - B

A - A

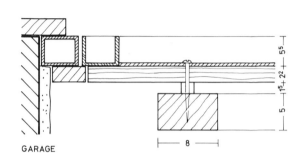

GARAGE

A - A

Ansicht und Grundriß 1:50   Elevation and ground plan 1:50
Schnitte 1:5   Sections 1:5

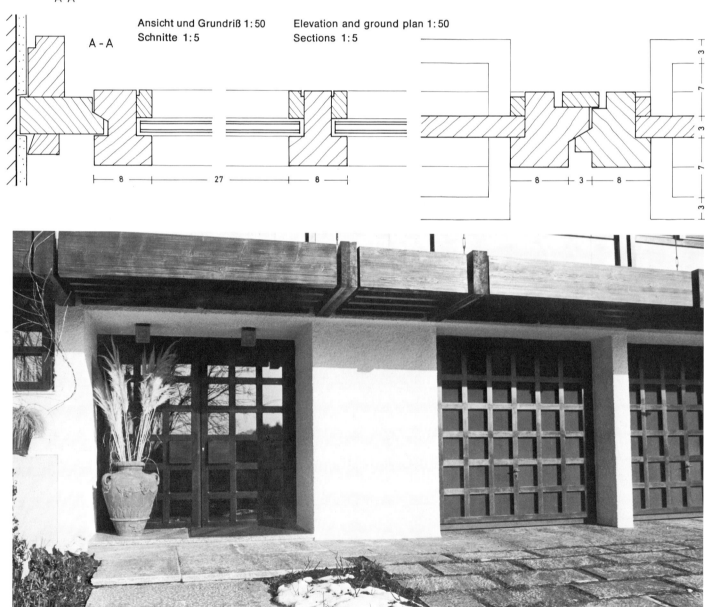

134

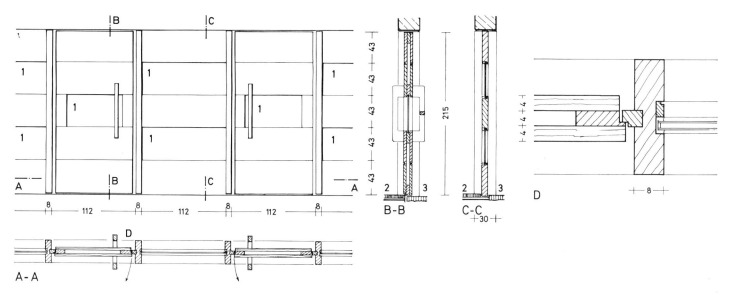

A-A

Ansicht, Grundriß und Schnitte 1:50, Detail 1:10

1 Glas
2 durchgehende Kokosmatte
3 Betonpflaster

Elevation, ground plan and sections 1:50, detail 1:10

1 Glass
2 Continuous coir matting
3 Concrete paving

Haupteingang der kath. Kirche in Korb. Rahmenkonstruktion, beidseitig mit Kieferndielen beplankt (verleimte Platten von 42 cm Breite), offenporiger dunkelbrauner Anstrich. Griffe Eiche, schwarz gebeizt. Türblattmaß 1,12 × 2,17 m. Anschlag mit Zapfenbändern, Bodentürschließer.

Architekten Kammerer + Belz, Stuttgart

Main entrance to the R. Cath. Church of Korb. Frame construction with pine boarding on both sides (glued, laminated panels 42 cm wide), open-pore paint coating in dark brown. Oak handle, stained black. Door leaf dimensions 1.12 × 2.17 m. Door stop with mortise hinges, floor closer.

Einfamilienhaus, Schorndorf. Die verhältnis-mäßig kleinen Räume werden durch das durchlaufende Oberlicht erweitert, der Flur gut belichtet. Türgröße 0,85 × 2,05 m. Türblatt Sperrholz, Kiefer furniert. Holzzarge. Verglasung 8–10 mm Tafelglas.

Innenarchitektin Helga Griese, Stuttgart
Architekt Fritz Vogt, Schorndorf

Private house, Schorndorf. The relatively small rooms are given a more spacious air by the continuous fanlight and well-lit hall. Door dimensions 0.85 × 2.05 m. Door leaf of plywood, with pine veneer. Door casing of wood. Overpanel glazing 8–10 mm sheet glass.

Wardrobe passage to bedroom. The room door as well as the cupboards are of sliding design. All woodwork is pine veneered. Ceiling lining solid pine.

Schrankflur vor dem Schlafzimmer. Die Zimmertür ist wie die Schranktüren als Schiebetür ausgebildet. Alles Holzwerk Kiefer furniert. Deckenverschalung Kiefer massiv.

Ansicht vom Schlafzimmer View from bedroom	Ansicht vom Flur View from passage	Ansicht vom Flur View from lobby

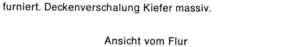

Wohnungseingang in Karlsruhe-Bergwald. Das Türblatt ist mit gekalkter Eiche furniert. Türgriff aus Aluminiumguß (Bildhauer R. A. Stiefvater, Freiburg).

Architekt Robert Düringer, Ihringen

Entrance to house in Karlsruhe-Bergwald. The door leaf is veneered with limed oak. Handle of cast aluminium (Sculptor R. A. Stiefvater, Freiburg).

Elevation and section 1:50
Details 1:5

1 Concrete with fair-faced masonry facing
2 Heraklith 60 mm
3 15 mm air cavity
4 Gypsum baseboard sheet, 1 cm
5 Plywood door leaf
6 Round steel bars, 20 mm, with
  2 threaded holes, dia. 6 mm
7 Door stop section, brass, continuous
  frame edging up to outer edge

Hauseingang an einem Einfamilienhaus in Krefeld. Das Sperrholz-Türblatt, 1,15 × 2,40 m groß, ist beidseitig mit Lärche furniert. Blockrahmen aus Kiefer, mit Spezialbeschlag an der Türschwelle befestigt.

Architekt Ernst Althoff, Krefeld

Entrance to detached house in Krefeld. The plywood door leaf, 1.15 × 2.40 m, is veneered on both sides with larch. Pine block frames with special door sill attachment.

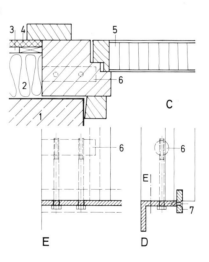

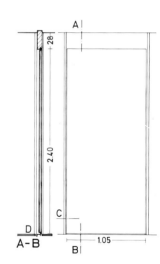

Ansicht und Schnitt 1:50
Details 1:5

1 Beton mit Sichtmauerwerk-Vorsatz
2 Heraklith 60 mm
3 15 mm Luft
4 Gipskarton-Platte 1 cm
5 Sperrholz-Türblatt
6 Rundstahl 20 mm, mit 2 Gewinde-
  löchern ⌀ 6 mm
7 Anschlagprofil, Messing, bis Außenkante Blendrahmen durchlaufend

Eingang zu einem Wohn- und Bürohaus in Stuttgart. Sperrholztür mit Kambala furniert. Das Türblatt, etwa 1,45 × 2,10 m groß, ist mit Zapfenbändern angeschlagen. Ihre Achse verläuft durch die kreisförmigen, mit Milchglas hinterlegten Lichtöffnungen. Der Türgriff aus Edelstahl ist neben dem Profilzylinder befestigt.

Architekt Paul Stohrer †

Entrance to a block of flats and offices in Stuttgart. Plywood door veneered with Kambala teak. The door leaf, approx. 1.45 × 2.10 m, is hung on mortise hinges. Their axis runs along the row of circular light apertures backed with milk glass. The stainless steel door knob is mounted at the side of the cylinder lock.

Einfamilienhaus in Hankensbüttel. Das Türblatt ist eine 28 mm Spanplatte, die zum Wohnraum mit Wenge, zum Flur mit Eiche furniert ist. Die Tür schlägt stumpf auf ein Zargenfutter; der seitliche Überstand verdeckt die Bänder und dient als Griffleiste. Auf der Flurseite ist eine Lederschlaufe als Griff angebracht. Zwei Magnetschnäpper halten die Tür geschlossen.

Architekt Otto Steinhöfel, Hankensbüttel

Private house in Hankensbuettel. The door leaf is of 28 mm coreboard, veneered with wengé on the living room side and with oak in the corridor. The door closes flush to the lining. The side projection conceals the hinges and the moulding serves as a door pull. On the corridor side a leather loop is attached to the handle. Two magnetic catches act as closers.

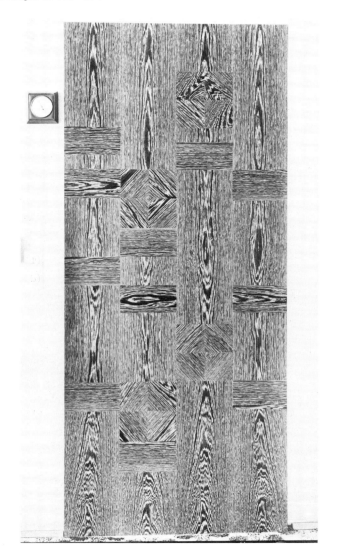

Verwaltungsgebäude des Süddeutschen Rundfunks, Stuttgart. Die Doppeltür des Haupteingangs ist mit Wenge furniert. Flügelmaß 1,05 × 2,20 m. Eingesetztes Sichtfeld aus Drahtfadenverbundglas; Griffplatten Aluminiumguß. Wandverkleidung über der Tür Kupferblech.

Architekten Rolf Gutbrod und Hermann Kiess, Stuttgart

Administration Building of the South German Broadcasting Station, Stuttgart. The double door of the main entrance is veneered with wengé. Wing dimensions 1.05 × 2.20 m. Inset panels of wired laminated glass; push plates of cast aluminium. Wall cladding over the door of copper sheet.

Altenheim des Caritasverbandes, Waiblingen. Die Türblätter des Haupteingangs sind aus Spanplatten, mit orangerot gebeiztem Ahorn furniert. Flügelmaß 1,12 × 2,18 m. Griffe Aluminium natur eloxiert. Rahmenkonstruktion Kiefer, dunkelbraun gestrichen.

Architekten Kammerer + Belz, Stuttgart

Old people's home of the Caritas Society, Waiblingen. The door leaves of the main entrance are of particle board panels veneered with maple, stained reddish-orange. Wing dimensions 1.12 × 2.18 m. Natural anodized aluminium handles. Framing system of pine, painted dark brown.

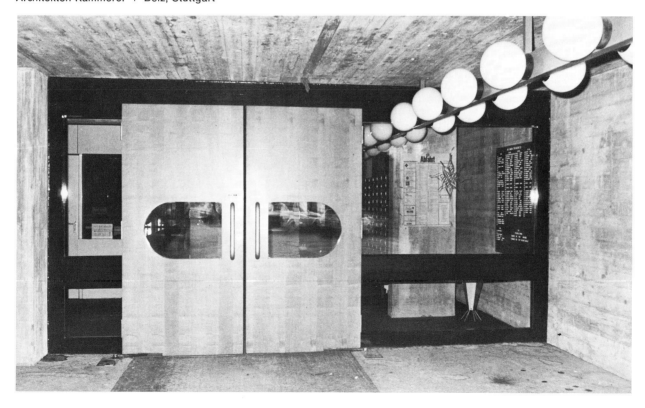

Kath. Kirche Kehlen. Die Türen besitzen eine Metall-Unterkonstruktion und sind mit Sperrholz bekleidet. Die plastisch ausgeformten Griffe und die Verstärkung des Türblatts in der Drehachse sind aus Massivholz. Alles Holz Hemlock, natur lasiert. Verglasungen aus Mehrscheiben-Panzerglas. Die Flügel sind außermittig gelagert. Türöffnung insgesamt 3,60 × 2,10 m. Die entsprechend konstruierte einflügelige Tür zur Sakristei mißt 1,05 × 2,10 m.

Architekten Kammerer + Belz, Stuttgart

R. Cath. Church, Kehlen. The doors have a metal core with plywood cladding. The plastic curved door pulls and the stiffening of the door leaf of the pivot hinge are of solid wood. All in hemlock, with transparent glaze. Laminated, armoured glass throughout. The wings are mounted off centre. Door opening altogether 3.60 × 2.10 m. The sacristy door is of similar construction, 1.05 × 2.10 m.

Eingangstür zu einem Privatclub in Mailand. Er liegt in den Arkaden der Innenstadt. Zwischen mit Spiegeln verglasten Feldern einer Schaufensterfront steht die Eingangstür von 1,40 × 2,20 m Größe. Ihre Außenseite ist wie das 0,85 m breite Feld links mit Palisander-Stäben 65 × 20 mm bekleidet. Die Innenseite wurde mit schwarzem Leder gepolstert. Der Name steht in Bronzebuchstaben in einem vertieften Oval, das im Seitenfeld als Fenster zur Besucherkontrolle ausgebildet ist („Spionspiegel"). Die Tür hat außen weder Schloß noch Griff, innen ist ein Zylinderschloß und eine Lederschlaufe angebracht.

Architekten Dr. Franco Bettonica und Dr. Gianfranco Frattini, Mailand

Entrance door to a private club in Milan, situated in the arcades of the town centre. The entrance door, 1.40 × 2.20 m, is set between plate glass shop windows. The door and the 0.85 m wide bay on the left have palisander strip cladding, 65 × 20 mm. The interior is upholstered in black leather. The name appears in bronze lettering on a recessed oval which has a side bay acting as a one-way vision panel to control visitors. The door has no lock or handle on the outside, there is a cylinder lock and leather loop on the inside only.

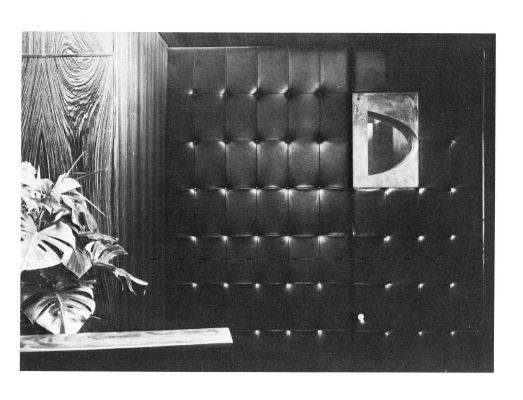

Institut für internationales und ausländisches Recht der Universität Köln. Die zweiflügelige Tür führt von der Eingangshalle zum Aufzugsvorraum. Konstruktion aus Stahlrohren, Füllungen aus Drahtspiegelglas mit davorgesetztem Raster aus Pag-Holz. Obentürschließer an beiden Flügeln.

Architekt Walther Ruoff, Köln

Institute for International and Foreign Law of the University of Cologne. The double-wing door leads from the entrance hall to the lift lobby. Tubular steel construction, panels of wired, polished plate glass with a front grid of jic-wood. Overhead closers on both wings.

Ansicht und Grundriß 1:20, Details 1:5

Elevation and ground plan 1:20. Details 1:5

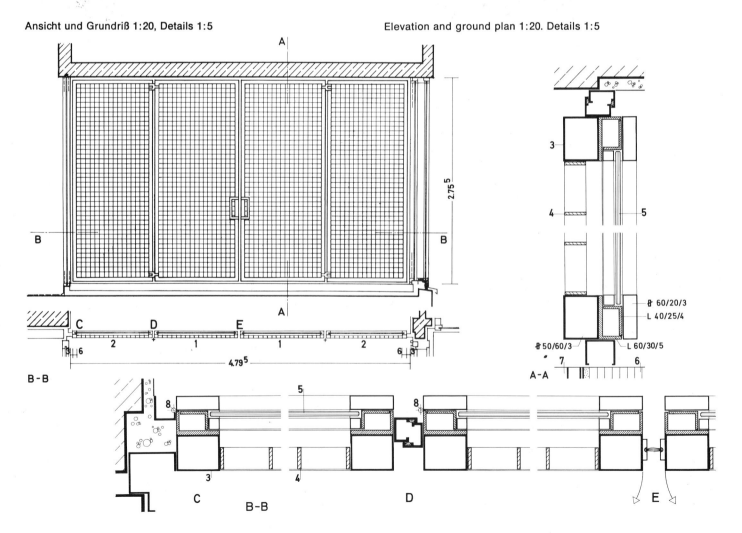

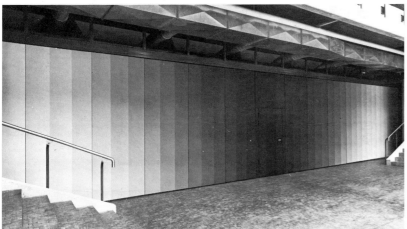

Berufschulzentrum Schwäbisch Gmünd. Die Falt-schiebewand zwischen Eingangsbereich und Aula ist 15,60 m breit und 3,26 m hoch. Sie besteht aus 13 Flügeln (Holzrahmenkonstruktion). Die Flächen sind in abgestuften Grautönen mit mattem Autolack ge-strichen. Jeder Flügel ist in 3 Felder geteilt, so daß sich 20 Abstufungen ergeben. Sie verlaufen auf der Eingangsseite (Foto oben) von Weiß über Schwarz nach Weiß, auf der Seite der Aula von Schwarz über Weiß nach Schwarz.

Farbgestaltung Arnulf Letto, Schwäbisch Gmünd
Architekten Roland Ostertag + Partner, Stuttgart

Vocational training centre, Schwaebisch Gmuend. The folding, sliding wall between the entrance area and the Assembly Hall is 15.60 m wide and 3.26 m high. It consists of 13 wings (wood framed construction). The surfaces are painted in graduated shades of grey with matt, car spray paint. Each wing is divided into 3 bays, to give 20 gradations. These pass from white to black to white on the entrance side and black to white to black on the hall side. The drums for the door wings remain mid-grey.

1 beweglicher Flügel
2 feststehendes Element
3 Türkonstruktion Stahlprofile
4 Gitter aus Preßholz
5 Spiegeldrahtglas, punktgeschweißt, 6—8 mm
6 Band zum Öffnen des Glasflügels zum Putzen
7 doppelte Bürste
8 Fußabstreifrost
9 Spaltklinker

◁

1 Swing wing
2 Fixed element
3 Door framing — steel sections
4 Grille of pressed wood
5 Wired, polished plate glass, dot welded, 6—8 mm
6 Hinge for opening the glazed wing for cleaning
7 Double brush
8 Foot scraper
9 Split clinker

Architekten und Künstler
architects and artists